SIMPLE.
NOT EASY.

Raj Ganpath is a certified coach and mentor with more than fifteen years of experience in the field of nutrition and fitness. He is a specialist in nutrition, strength training, biomechanics, women's fitness, functional training, kettlebell training and core conditioning, in addition to being certified in senior fitness and Olympic lifting. He has enabled tens of thousands of Indians around the world to change their lives for the better by helping them get fit, lose weight and improve their health.

He is widely recognised for his work in simplifying complex fitness and nutrition concepts and helping apply them practically. Every day, he teaches people how they can simplify their lives by taking the mystery out of fitness and nutrition, and helping them make better choices for a stronger life.

Raj is also an entrepreneur and one of the founders of Quad Fitness, where his team of passionate coaches work with thousands of everyday people from around the world and help them look, feel and function better in life.

When he addresses an audience, coaches a class, posts on social media, teaches a workshop or mentors his team, Raj strives to do the one thing—simplify fitness in order to make it accessible, approachable and attainable by anyone.

SIMPLE,
NOT EASY

A NO-NONSENSE GUIDE TO FITNESS, NUTRITION AND WEIGHT LOSS

RAJ GANPATH

Published by Westland Books, a division of Nasadiya Technologies Private Limited, in 2025

No. 269/2B, First Floor, 'Irai Arul', Vimalraj Street, Nethaji Nagar, Alapakkam Main Road, Maduravoyal, Chennai 600095

Westland and the Westland logo are the trademarks of Nasadiya Technologies Private Limited, or its affiliates.

Copyright © Raj Ganpath, 2025

Raj Ganpath asserts the moral right to be identified as the author of this work.

ISBN: 9789360453725

10 9 8 7 6 5 4 3 2 1

The views and opinions expressed in this work are the author's own and the facts are as reported by him, and the publisher is in no way liable for the same.

All rights reserved

Typeset by Jojy Philip

Printed at Thomson Press

No part of this book may be reproduced, or stored in a retrieval system, or transmitted in any form or by any means, electronic, mechanical, photocopying, recording, or otherwise, without express written permission of the publisher.

To Calvin.
Words will never suffice.

Contents

Introduction — xiii

SECTION 1: THE BIG PICTURE — 1

#1 Fitness is an ability, not a look or a feat — 2

#2 Fitness is a problem you solve every day — 4

#3 Fitness is not just for fit people — 6

#4 Fitness is an infinite game — 8

#5 Purpose drives progress — 10

#6 Start by subtracting — 12

#7 Simplify — 14

SECTION 2: NUTRITION — 17

#8 Food is more than just fuel — 18

#9 We live in an age of abundance — 21

#10 Mindfulness matters — 23

#11 Mindfulness begins with awareness — 25

#12 Trust your body — 27

#13 The trick is to pay attention — 29

#14 The only way to overcome 'food guilt' — 31

#15 Experience food without judgement — 34

#16 The practical nutrition framework — 36

#17 Health, strength, comfort, luxury and fun — 39

#18 Mindless eating—the guaranteed way to ill health — 41

#19 Start by building a smart plate of food — 43

#20 Food quantity matters — 47

#21 Eat as well as you can, but only as much as necessary — 49

#22 Satisfied or stuffed? — 51

#23 Knowing when to stop is a skill — 53

#24 The faster you eat, the more you eat — 55

#25 Slow down — 57

#26 The more often you eat, the more mistakes you make — 59

#27 It doesn't matter when — 62

#28 The incredible Indian diet — 64

#29 If it is homemade, it is healthy — 67

#30 Use, don't abuse — 69

#31 Simplicity presents itself before and after complexity — 72

SECTION 3: MOVEMENT — 75

#32 Movement is mandatory — 76

#33 The three types of movement — 79

#34 Anyone can exercise, and everyone should exercise — 81

#35 The four Ss of exercise — 83

#36 Strength makes you better — 85

#37 Strength training simplified — 87

#38 The three commandments of strength training — 91

#39 Do it well or don't do it at all — 93

#40 Stamina is what keeps you going — 95

#41 The different types of endurance — 97

#42 Embrace discomfort, build stamina — 100

#43 Speed and power — 102

#44 Training for speed and power — 104

#45 To be strong, you need to be supple — 107

#46 Supple enough — 109

#47 Structure your training, one week at a time — 111

#48 The 10,000-step solution — 114

SECTION 4: SLEEP — 117

#49 Sleep is when the magic happens — 118

#50 Tired but wired   121

#51 Comfortable, cold, dark and quiet   123

#52 The rhythm we all dance to   126

#53 Harness the power of light   128

#54 It's warm, brown and bitter, but it makes your brain 'brain' better   130

#55 Coffee—use it, don't abuse it   132

#56 Doing the right thing at the wrong time   134

#57 Not too late, not too much   136

#58 Get triggered   138

#59 How much sleep is enough sleep?   140

#60 Simplifying sleep   142

#61 Damage control   145

SECTION 5: STRESS   149

#62 There is no growth without stress   150

#63 The two types of stress   153

#64 Stop, listen and become aware   155

#65 Tolerance is a skill   157

#66 Is there good and bad stress?   160

#67 Stress management 101   162

#68 Breathe your way to better health   164

SECTION 6: WEIGHT LOSS   169

#69 We all care about how we look, and there's nothing wrong with that   170

#70 Your body doesn't want you to lose weight   173

#71 What you really want is 'fat loss'   175

#72 The first law of thermodynamics   177

#73 Calories in, calories out   179

#74 In a world of abundance, a shortage is what we need   182

#75 Move more, do more, burn more   185

#76 Build more muscle, burn more calories   188

#77 A very short summary of how to burn more calories   190

#78 Restrict yourself, mindfully and consistently   192

#79 The science of 'calories'   194

#80 Weight loss using a framework   196

#81 Weight loss using a strategy   198

#82 Weight loss using rules   201

#83 Weight loss using diets   204

#84 Not maximal. Not minimal. Optimal — 206

#85 Save what you need, burn what you don't — 208

#86 Embrace hunger — 210

#87 Why do some people lose weight faster than others? — 213

#88 Pills, potions and procedures — 216

#89 Weight loss in ten simple actions — 219

SECTION 7: CONSISTENCY — 223

#90 It all adds up — 224

#91 Betterment is the goal — 226

#92 Are you uncomfortable enough? — 228

#93 Motivation wanes but habits compound — 230

#94 Consistency is a life skill — 233

#95 Mastering consistency — 236

#96 Moderation is an expert move — 239

#97 Patience. Consistency. Resilience. — 241

#98 Be clear. Be confident. Be consistent. — 243

#99 Back yourself — 245

#100 In a nutshell — 247

Introduction

Why should you read this book?

This is not a typical diet book. You will not find meal plans, nutrition charts or calorie recommendations. This is not a typical exercise book either. So you will not find images of exercises, hacks and tricks to lose weight, methods to get you to extreme fitness or make you an absolute beast.

This book is an unusual mix of science, reason and positivity, and it is meant to simplify, provide clarity and inspire action. Because, fitness, while certainly not easy, can be very simple. And, once simplified, it becomes much easier for you to put in the right effort needed to achieve your goals without confusion, hesitation or FOMO.

We are all smart in our own ways. While not all of us have the time or patience to decode technical concepts, look up jargon and make sense of scientific experiments, we can understand logic and reasoning almost instantly. If something makes sense, if it seems logical, we tend to understand it. If something doesn't sound quite right, we have a natural urge to question it. So, instead of overloading you with data and facts, I am going to appeal to your rational side and humbly request your sensibility. And together, we're going to try to understand this seemingly confusing and complicated world of fitness by asking 'why'.

Because I truly believe that if you can understand something, you don't have to remember it. When the *why* is simplified and understood, it provides clarity on the *what* and will guide you to figure out the *how*, which will, without doubt, lead to progress.

When I started working on this book, I had a simple mission—to make this worth your while. I am deeply grateful that you have chosen to invest some of your hard-earned money and valuable time in this book. And I want to make sure that it is worth it. So, this book will contain

- No big words, no jargon and no confusing language. I have purposely written this book using simple words and short chapters. Because my goal is to communicate and not complicate. If at the end of each short chapter you feel a sense of clarity and confidence, that's a win. And if you are able to get through this entire book without having to look up even a single word, that's a bigger win.
- No long chapters and no beating around the bush. Instead, you'll find a set of 100 short and easy-to-read chapters, each addressing a relevant and important aspect of fitness in a simple and—hopefully—memorable manner.
- No fearmongering. As much as social media will disagree, the world is not filled with food-related perils. While it is necessary to be mindful, there is no reason to be paranoid. So I have been careful in ensuring that this book is geared towards creating awareness and positivity and not fear and anxiety. In fact, the word 'danger' appears in this book exactly one time—now.
- Simple, clear and positive information at every stage and on every page. Because my larger goal is to make you feel confident that fitness is something that is accessible and attainable.

But before we move on, please allow me a moment to thank you. For your time. For your interest in fitness and science. For wanting to be a better version of yourself. And for choosing to see the big picture instead of looking for quick fixes and shortcuts.

Because this is not just about you. You may be an engineer designing and building the future. Or a doctor saving lives. Or a teacher, mentor, coach or leader shaping the minds of the present and the future. Or a parent, homemaker or caregiver who is responsible for other lives every day. By taking care of yourself, you will look, feel and function better, which will help you do whatever you do better. This will make the people around you happier and that, in some small way, will make the world around you a better place. So, thank you.

Who am I, and why am I writing this book?

My journey with fitness started when I was twenty-five years old. Like many of you reading this, I started late. I was not an athlete in school and didn't really play a sport or do anything very active in my early years. In fact, I was very inactive and unfit up until the day I decided I didn't want to be that anymore.

As a young kid, I loved to play. But I didn't play much because I was severely asthmatic. I still vividly remember my first asthma attack. I was ten years old and had my first karate class after school. We were asked to run a few rounds around the school ground to warm up. I ran like all the other kids did. But after my first round, I suddenly found it hard to breathe. This was an unfamiliar feeling and it scared me. I stopped, sat down on the curb and started crying. I was out of breath, scared, frustrated and embarrassed all at once. I can still feel that sensation as I type this out. I had to sit out of class. But in an hour or so, I felt better and moved on to the next distraction, like any ten-year-old would.

From then on, this became a regular occurrence in my life. I figured out the pattern—if I exerted myself or was exposed to dust, I got an attack. So, as a pre-teen, I did the most obvious thing—staying away from activity and allergens. And this was my life for the next fifteen years, through school, college, university and work. My parents, who were and are always caring and supportive, tried every treatment available back then. But there was no cure in sight. The best I could do was manage the condition by using an inhaler when I had an attack.

I moved from Chennai in Tamil Nadu, South India (my hometown) to Pilani in Rajasthan, North India (for college) and then to New Jersey in the Northeastern United States (for my Master's) and then to California in the Western United States (for work). But, irrespective of the weather and environment, the asthma didn't improve, and neither did my fitness.

In 2008, I went through a very bad phase in my life. I had physiological, professional and emotional issues all at once. It was too much to handle. It crushed me. I spiralled and got to a point where I was pushing myself down the spiral even more. One day, and I clearly remember this moment, I walked across my room and caught my reflection in the mirror. It was a rude shock and a reality check. I did not look anything like myself. I had gained a lot of weight, had a prominent frown and looked like someone who had completely lost the plot.

Now, I'm not someone who makes resolutions or looks for turning points in life. But at that moment, I decided that I was going to turn things around for myself. I decided to use all the frustration and angst I had in me to fuel myself to do better. I decided to create something positive out of all this negativity. Instead of destroying myself, I swore to rebuild myself. And so my journey started.

I started with running, because it was the one thing I could never do. No matter where or how old I was, if I ran, I'd have an asthma attack in a matter of seconds. So I wanted to slay this demon. I thought if I could do that, it would give me the confidence to do bigger and better things. So I wore whatever clothes and shoes I had and headed out at about 9 p.m. on a crisp October night in Mountain View, California. I started running. And, unsurprisingly, within a minute, I had an attack. I sat down on the curb—a spot I was used to by this time in my life. I took a hit of the bronchodilator, which usually opens up my airways and allows me to breathe. I looked back and realised that I covered less than a hundred metres.

I've been in this position many times in my life. But this time, I did one thing differently—I got up and ran again. In another hundred-odd metres, I had another attack. I sat down, rested, took another hit, got up and ran again. I did this over and over again and ended up running about 900 metres in close to an hour. It was terrible. But I knew something had changed. I felt it. And after that night, I ran every night. It sucked. But it sucked less and less as the days progressed.

Despite having no idea about nutrition, I made some basic changes to what I ate. Back then, my coffees were sweet lattes, I was eating fast food seven to ten times a week, every meal had a bag of chips and at least half a litre of cola and I was eating purely for taste and comfort. I reduced fast food to two or three times a week, halved the chips and dumped the cola, ate more berries and vegetables and just ate less in general. It seemed to work and the scale was responding.

After about three months of this, I tried my first distance run. To my surprise, I covered 14 miles! But the asthma was still there and so was the inhaler in my pocket. What changed was when and how frequently I would get the attack and my learning of how to use it before things got very bad. So, I ran more and more. I got to a point where I was running about 100 kilometres every week. In about seven months, I had lost a little more than 50 pounds (about 23 kilos). I didn't look 'fat' anymore and was fairly happy. This got me interested in understanding the human body better and I decided to 'study' fitness and nutrition more deeply.

It was only then that I realised I had made a mistake. Because I had lost a lot of weight by doing mostly cardio and reducing food, I had ended up being 'skinny fat', where I was skinny but had lost a lot of muscle too. As a result, I was weak and flabby. Some basic research helped me understand why this happened and that the way around this was strength training and balanced nutrition. So I began lifting weights, sprinting, learning skills like kickboxing, including callisthenics and plyometrics, and experimenting with a variety of diets.

I was loving it. This newfound interest in learning flipped many switches in my head. At this point it was starting to become clear that I had a strong pull towards this field. I dove head first into exercise and nutrition science. I dedicated all my time before and after work and during the weekends for research. I spent hours reading and researching every day, understanding the basics and the specifics. I got my first certification. And I set out to figure out the cause of my asthma and hopefully find a cure.

With enough research, I realised my asthma could be a result of a food allergy or intolerance. So, I started tinkering with what I ate. I removed this, added that, tried this, replaced that and kept iterating for months. Finally, I realised that I had food intolerances, specifically gluten, dairy and shellfish, which had a big impact on my respiration and affected how easily, quickly, frequently and intensely I got my attacks.

Considering this was a time when the connection between nutrition, gut integrity and health was not commonly discussed or understood, this was surprising and exciting for me. I dug deeper into nutrition—the science behind it, the anecdotal evidence that was not backed by science, the extent of its influence on our physical and mental health and, most importantly, the practical application of all of this.

I understood how powerful movement and nutrition can be in improving a person's life. But I also realised that not everyone would have the luxury of time or interest to go deep into nutrition science as I did. And so I decided I wanted to study and understand nutrition, movement, stress and sleep as well as possible so I could simplify it for people like me, who want to and deserve to have a better quality of life.

Once I had this clarity, there was no turning back. I started working with people on their fitness while I was working a full-time job in R&D in the medical device industry. And everyone I worked with experienced incredible results. This led to more certifications, more research and more hours of experimenting, learning and teaching. It was around this time that I met my current business partner Arvind Ashok, who was on a similar journey of his own. Our vision aligned—we wanted to make a deep impact in people's lives by helping them look, feel and function better. And so we decided to make the biggest switch of our lives—career, country and lifestyle.

The next couple of years were all about prep—training, meeting great coaches, trying different programmes and doing more and more research. And in 2011, we gave up our lives in California, moved back home and founded The Quad in Chennai, India. We went from being the typical nine-to-six desk job workers in the US making more money that we needed, driving fun cars, enjoying weekends and complaining about Mondays, to becoming fitness coaches and entrepreneurs in India, waking up at 3.30 a.m., passionately working with hundreds of wonderful people, making mistakes, struggling with our lifestyles, learning, improving, striving to make a difference and absolutely loving it.

From then on, I have had one simple but consistent goal guiding me at every step: 'be useful'. This has been my north star and, for seventeen years now, it has inspired and enabled me to design programmes, structure plans, write blogs and columns, give talks and lectures, conduct workshops, run classes, mentor nutrition and fitness coaches and help improve the lives of thousands of people just like me and you. With the same goal in mind, and with immeasurable amounts of help, support and encouragement from my co-founder, family, friends and team, I have also built an honest and passionate fitness organisation and helped create an inclusive and non-judgemental community of like-minded people.

Today, after all these years, my passion for fitness and interest in science have only grown, and my north star still shines bright. And this book is another step towards the same goal of being useful and helping people change their lives for the better. Because, from experience, experimentation and expertise, I know for a fact that fitness can drastically change one's life for the better, and for that one reason, it is worth a lifetime of striving, learning and teaching.

How to read this book?

I've written this book with simplicity and practicality as the primary goals. So, while there will be a few specifics, the majority of the book will deal with the big picture and practical application of theoretical concepts. In other words, the majority of the book will deal with simplifying deep and complex matters to a point where they are easily understandable by everyone. But the realisations that occur will undeniably be deep and impactful.

So, I urge you to not read this book like any other book, in one shot or in long sittings. Instead, I recommend that you read a chapter or two, spend time internalising it and understanding how it is relevant to your life and then come back for more.

Treat this book as your guide and don't try to finish it. Because every day you read this book, you will learn something about yourself and give yourself an opportunity to prioritise your fitness, your lifestyle and yourself.

Don't rush it. Take your time. Read, understand, introspect, rationalise and, most importantly, apply.

SECTION 1

THE BIG PICTURE

#1 Fitness is an ability, not a look or a feat

Modern fitness evolved from earlier versions of physical fitness. Earlier, strongmen, bodybuilders, athletes and models were the ones who spent time thinking about or doing anything related to exercise and nutrition. Words like 'quadriceps' and 'calorie deficit' were not part of the common person's vocabulary. Neither were terms like 'resveratrol', 'gut integrity', 'VO2 max', 'mobility' or 'intermittent fasting'. This is not the case anymore.

Fitness has become a familiar topic for many across different ages, genders, sizes, ethnicities and cultures. In a world where convenience wins and movement has been reduced to 'do only when necessary', fitness has moved from being a choice to a necessity. From a 'nice to have' to a 'must have'. Because, in order to live a purposeful, happy and healthy life, we need to satisfy our unique needs and wants. If we're able to do that, we feel stimulated and excited. We thrive. But when we are unable to, we find ourselves stressed and exhausted. We struggle. This is why the definition of fitness varies drastically based on each person's specific needs and wants.

Fitness is an ability. Not just a look, feat or metric. All of us need this ability to varying extents depending on who we are, what we do and what roles we play in our respective lives.

And that's why fitness is not defined based on your body fat percentage or how much weight you can lift or how fast you can run. Instead, fitness is defined as the ability

- to maintain a state of well-being free of pain and disease
- to carry out daily tasks without undue fatigue
- to function efficiently in an active environment that suits your personal interests and goals

For a professional tennis player, fitness is about performance. It is the ability to sustain many hours of running, aiming, hitting and recovering soon enough to do all of this over and over again.

For a neurosurgeon, fitness is the ability to stay strong, calm, focused and precise even during times of extreme pressure and fatigue.

For a teacher, fitness is the ability to stand for hours, teach with energy and passion and be patient and caring to the hundreds of children they engage with.

For all of us, fitness is the ability to do what we *need* to do and *want* to do in *our* unique lives, while keeping disease, disability and pain as far away as possible.

Fitness is not just about aesthetics and performance for everyone. It is about looking, feeling and functioning better every day.

> What are the things you 'need' to do in your life? Do you currently have the fitness to do all these things?
>
> What are the things you 'want' in your life? Do you want to travel, dance, play a sport, look a certain way, work without fatigue, live without pain? What form and level of fitness do you think you need in order to achieve these things?

#2 Fitness is a problem you solve every day

We tend to be too hard on ourselves when it comes to health and fitness. We swear to eat well and exercise regularly. When we succeed, we feel proud. It makes our day. We experience a sense of achievement, and we feel hopeful and in control. When we fail, we feel terrible. It breaks our day. We experience guilt and feel depressed.

What if we were a little kinder to ourselves? Wouldn't it be wonderful to remove the extreme feelings and self-judgement? What does it take to be calmer about our efforts and less volatile with our emotions? Clarity.

And the clarity we need is actually a realisation that fitness is a problem that we need to solve one day at a time, for the rest of our lives. There is no start, there is no end and there is no rush. One good day or week won't produce any great results, and one bad day or week won't spoil it all.

Say you had a great day yesterday. You exercised, ate properly, stayed active and took care of yourself well. That's wonderful. But this morning, the slate is clean. And you need to do it all over again.

Say you had a terrible day yesterday. You didn't move much, you gave in to temptations and ate too much. That's OK. Don't beat yourself up. Because this morning, the slate is wiped clean. And you get another shot at this whole fitness thing.

Irrespective of who you are—young or old, big or small, professional or amateur, male or female, beginner or big celebrity—fitness is something you need to work on every day. So, forget yesterday, however positive or negative it was. What's done is done. Today is a brand-new day, and you have a brand-new opportunity to build a better you.

> Do you think that the effort you need to put in to improve your fitness (or lose weight or build strength) is time bound and temporary? Or have you realised that irrespective of how much you progress, you'll need to continue working on your fitness for the rest of your life?

#3 Fitness is not just for fit people

Consider all the new training programmes and equipment released in the market. Most, if not all, are meant to 'supercharge' your training or 'take your results to the next level'. Essentially, they are meant to make fit people even fitter.

Think about all the advertisements you see. For supplements, equipment and clothing. And the models used in them. The look, fit, feel and vibe of these advertisements resonate with and inspire some people—those who are already fit or are already on their fitness journeys. But do they really make fitness accessible and less intimidating for people who aren't?

And look at most of the famous fitness accounts on social media. They are filled with flex, feats and perfectly angled selfies. They drive home the narrative that fitness is about looking a certain way or doing impressive physical feats. They are fun to watch. But they make millions of people feel ashamed about how they look and demotivated about their progress. Because the hidden subtle message in all of this is that fitness is for fit people. And that is not OK.

The problem here is that this is a message of the past. It is from a time when fitness was relevant only for people who needed to be extremely fit—athletes, bodybuilders, strongmen, dancers. Or for those who had to showcase their fitness, such as actors, models, celebrities.

This was also a time when movement was a bigger and more regular part of people's everyday lives. Basic fitness was something that most people had. A couple of generations back, people had enough everyday strength and stamina to lift heavy things, run, jump, crawl, lunge, push, pull and walk for hours. Anything beyond this was not necessary for general health. It was only for performance or presentation.

We live in a different time now. Our lives have become more convenient and comfortable. We don't have the time or the necessity to move as often as before. We don't move. And so we don't have the everyday fitness of the people from the past.

Today, fitness has become a basic requirement for life, relevant and necessary for anyone, irrespective of profession, sex, gender, age or nationality. And this is why fitness is for everyone today. Especially for those who are not fit enough and for those who have not begun their fitness journey yet.

So, remember, fitness is NOT only for fit people. And the point of fitness is not just to become skinny, build big muscles, lift the most weight or get ripped. Fitness is for everyone. And the point of fitness is actually betterment.

> Take a moment to reflect—what are your current fitness goals? Are they aesthetic or functional in nature? And more importantly, what roles do you play in life? And how can improving your fitness help you in each of these roles?

#4 Fitness is an infinite game

Most of us consider fitness as something finite. We think about losing X kilos in the next Y months. We want to train for a marathon. We sign up for twelve-week programmes. We hope to transform ourselves in a few months. While all these feel complete, they are time bound, temporary and only a small part of a much larger journey.

Fitness is a never-ending game. Like parenting, business, education and life itself, there is no manual or rulebook. There isn't one set of rules that applies to everyone. The game was being played before you started and will continue after you stop. And the goal of the game is not to win. It is to keep playing, keep learning and keep discovering new levels and experiences.

Fitness is not something you can 'finish'. It is a lifelong pursuit. Because reaching a 'goal' is not the end. It is just a milestone that marks the end of one bout of effort and signifies the start of the next. And that's why fitness needs to be fun, purposeful and sustainable for it to make sense in the long term.

So start viewing fitness as a never-ending journey of betterment. You'll realise that there is no rush. You'll realise that you have the rest of your life to get stronger, leaner and healthier. You'll realise what you can achieve is truly limitless. Because an infinite game comes with infinite possibilities.

Think about the last ten or twenty years of your life. What are all the things you have done in an effort to improve your fitness during these years? Think about all the diets, programmes, supplements, cleanses, competitions, classes and challenges you have been a part of.

Think about the next ten or twenty years of your life. Do you see yourself continuing to work on your health and fitness? Do you see an end or a finish line after which you don't have to be active or make healthier food choices?

#5 Purpose drives progress

Fitness is not free or cheap. It requires investment—time, money and effort. You need to put in a lot: over 200 hours a year, many thousands of rupees every month and plenty of effort, most of which is discomfort. Practically speaking, you wouldn't invest so much into anything unless you had a strong reason to.

So, in all seriousness, why do you want to invest so much of your life into this? Why do you want to improve your fitness?

The answer to this question can't be simple. 'Oh, I just want to lose some weight' or 'Everyone is doing it and so . . . ' or even 'I just want to be in better health' won't cut it. The reason needs to be clear and strong. So clear that it should make sense to you on any day. And so strong that it should get you to do the work even when you just don't feel like doing it.

Because *purpose is the driving force behind progress.*

All will seem well at the start, when things are moving smoothly. But with time, the going will get tough. Life will catch up. Priorities will change. You will find it harder and harder to stay consistent. You will get to a point where you don't see results. Slowly but surely, the investment will start to seem too big or disproportionate. And eventually, you'll find a stronger reason to not pursue fitness than to unsuccessfully keep chipping away at it. Because without a strong purpose, progress will always be a struggle.

But if you have a clear and strong purpose, it will drive you to keep doing the work. Even when you are not motivated. Even when life gets hard. Even when results aren't obvious. You will make it happen. Somehow.

This is the secret behind consistency. And this is the reason you need to identify and internalise your 'why' and use it to drive you forward. When the going gets tough. When self-doubt creeps in. When you are about to lose that fire in you.

Purpose. It makes everything possible.

> How much do you invest in your fitness? Can you quickly add up all the time and money you spend towards your fitness every month? What about the effort? Consider food prep, commute, muscle burn, high heart rates, soreness, injuries, etc.
>
> What is your 'why'? What is the purpose behind improving your fitness? Is it clear to you? Is it strong enough to drive you to keep doing the work in the long term?

#6 Start by subtracting

Fitness revolves around DOs and DONTs. Every 'do' is something you add to your life. And every 'don't' is something you remove from your life.

Addition is exciting. It provides newness. It brings new experiences and possibilities. Doing more makes you feel like you are actively working towards a goal. You have something to show as effort. Adding exercise to your day or protein to your meals in an effort to lose fat is an example.

On the other side of excitement is exhaustion. Adding to a full plate or adding too many things could result in feeling overwhelmed. This is more common than you would think. In fact, most people who start their fitness journeys tend to get overwhelmed in a few weeks. They either throw in the towel or put in subpar effort, resulting in little to no progress.

Subtraction, on the other hand, is not fun. Especially when you have to remove something you enjoy. But subtraction helps create space and time. You may feel a sense of deprivation. But that can be dealt with through smart replacement, especially when you have more time and space.

Reducing how often you binge-eat is an example. As you reduce the frequency of binge nights, you reward yourself with more energy and time and less lethargy and guilt. This will invariably result in positive feelings of self, which will result in an increased drive to do better. That, in turn, will result in consistency, which will result in progress.

So, start by subtracting. Instead of adding more things to do in your day, smartly remove the things that are holding you back. Because when you have fewer things to do, you have the time and space to do them better.

Not easy. But certainly simple. Try it.

> Do you prefer adding or subtracting? When you think about improving your health or fitness, do you immediately think about things to do or not do?
>
> If you had to remove or reduce three things from your life that will enable you to improve your health or fitness, what would they be?

#7 Simplify

Fitness can be complicated, confusing and intimidating. Because there are too many options. Too many programmes. Too many diets. Too many magic bullets. And too many opinions.

It is true that there is no one way to get fit. Or lose weight, build strength or improve your stamina. But that doesn't justify trying everything or doing more and more.

The allure of more is hard to resist. And that's because we have been taught that 'more is better'. If five exercises can help build strength, then ten should help build more strength. If 2 kilos of weight loss a month is good, then 5 kilos should be better, and so on.

In reality, you can do a lot better with less. And simplification is the path to less. Because simplification reduces the number of variables and moving parts you need to deal with at any given point of time. And with fewer moving parts, you can consistently devote more attention to the ones that truly matter.

Strength? There are thousands of exercises out there. But, simplify and just work on the basics regularly for a couple of years. I guarantee a much stronger version of you.

Endurance? There are innumerable ways to improve it. But, simplify and just walk, run, cycle or play sports consistently. Progress will be inevitable.

Nutrition? A range of diets, plans, concepts and theories are available. But, simplify and just maximise protein and vegetables and minimise sweet and fatty foods. You'll be shocked to see how well your body weight, body composition and health markers improve.

Whatever it is you are after, simple will do it. It might feel like you're missing out on something. It might seem like you are doing the bare minimum. It might even feel like you are progressing slower than the others. But rest assured that the simpler you make it, the longer you'll do it. And the longer you do it, the fitter you will become.

So, simplify. Simplify everything. And simplify everything brutally.

> Consider two aspects of your life—movement and nutrition. Think of everything you do to work on these aspects. How can you simplify? What would you subtract? And once you do that, how much time and mental space would it open up for you?
>
> Are you willing to try a simplified version of what you're doing for the next few months?

SECTION 2

NUTRITION

#8 Food is more than just fuel

We talk so much about nutrition—what to eat, food composition, calories and so on. But nutrition is about a very basic need—energy and nutrients.

Theoretically, nutrition is about consuming foods that contain energy and nutrients that are necessary for health and growth.

We all need energy and nutrients to live, grow and reproduce. Not just us but every animal and plant too. Without energy, nothing is possible. Our bodies need energy to perform the most basic tasks, including respiration, blood circulation, cell formation and even making and breaking bonds between atoms inside cells. Most of us understand this.

But what about nutrients? There are nutrients we need in large amounts, aka macronutrients or macros. And nutrients we need in small amounts, aka micronutrients or micros.

Carbohydrates, fats and proteins are the macronutrients. They provide us with the building blocks of our bodies—glucose, fatty acids and amino acids. They also provide us with energy. Every gram of carbohydrate and protein provides us with 4 kcal. And every gram of fat provides us with 9 kcal. We need enough of all three macronutrients for us to thrive. Not too much and not too little, just enough. And 'enough' varies from person to person based on a multitude of factors.

Vitamins and minerals are the micronutrients. We need thirteen vitamins and over seventy minerals. These are required in very small amounts, and they don't provide us with energy. But they are fundamentally necessary for health. Any deficiency can result in ill-health and even life-threatening conditions. Just like macronutrients, we need 'enough' of these micronutrients too. And here too, 'enough' varies from person to person.

But, is this all nutrition is? Do we need to treat food as fuel? Mechanically ensure we're getting enough of everything? Surely not.

Because, *practically, nutrition is about consuming foods that help us grow healthier and stronger while keeping us comfortable and allowing us to enjoy some luxury and fun.*

Because food is more than just fuel. It used to be just fuel. And for many animals in the wild, it still is. But if you're reading this, chances are you're past the 'food is for survival' stage. You're probably at the 'food is an emotion' stage. And that's OK. Because food today is many things. It is fuel too, of course. But food is also something that helps us 'feel'.

What we call 'taste' is actually a combination of different sensory inputs—smell, texture, temperature and, of course, taste itself. We have taste buds, with many sensors, that help us make sense of what we're eating and whether it is 'good' or 'bad'. This information makes eating safe and pleasurable. This, in turn, encourages us to seek food, because the brain is hardwired to seek pleasure.

If there is no pleasure in eating, there is a high chance that we won't eat. This will result in a lack of energy and nutrients, which will in turn result in the death of the being and the extinction of the species. Evolution does not want that to happen.

This is why we love food. This is why we feel so many emotions around food. This is also why we salivate at the sight or even thought of some of our favourite foods—the brain remembers the pleasure from the last time you ate those foods and encourages you to eat them again. The temptation and pull you feel towards food is much more a part of your being that you can imagine.

This is why we eat. Not just to stop feeling hungry, but also to feel happy.

And this is why food can't be just fuel. It has to not just nourish, but also please.

And this is precisely why we need to think of food not only as something that enables health and growth, but also something that gives us comfort and happiness.

> What does food mean to you? Do you eat only when you're hungry? Or do you eat for reasons other than hunger? Do you struggle to control the urge to eat more?

… # #9 We live in an age of abundance

If pleasure is such a big part of eating, then how can we protect ourselves from overeating? What stops us from giving in to pleasure? Why shouldn't we eat whatever we want, whenever we want and how much ever we want?

Our wants are always more than our needs. This applies to food as much as it does to anything else in life. And the struggle is balancing what you need to eat and what you want to eat. This is because, today, we live in an age of abundance. While food scarcity still exists in parts of the world, most people suffer with health and body weight issues today due to abundance and not due to scarcity.

The reason for this struggle is simple. Our bodies were designed to navigate through a world where food was not easily available. But today, food is available in abundance, at any time and with minimal effort—all it needs is a few clicks on your favourite food app! This mismatch, where we are fundamentally wired to seek out more food (and pleasure) but, at the same time, we are in need of consciously restraining ourselves from overconsuming, is the problem pretty much everyone reading this is dealing with today.

Over the centuries, we have crafted many methods to deal with this mismatch. While these methods seem drastically different from one another, conscious and voluntary restriction of food is the basic idea behind all of them. Because there is simply no way around it.

As mentioned before, we need 'just enough' food, energy and nutrients. When food was scarce, we got to 'just enough' by doing everything we could to source, prepare and consume as much food as possible. Even after all our efforts, we barely got what we needed. But now, when food is abundant, the only way to get to 'just enough' is through conscious and voluntary restriction.

> Is food abundance a problem for you? How do we restrict ourselves optimally so we are able to stay healthy and happy? Do you think restriction without deprivation is possible?

#10   Mindfulness matters

Consider all the methods of restriction we have come up with. Most of them work only in the very short term—a few weeks. Some work for a little longer, maybe a few months. But only very few work in the long term.

What we have learnt is that the more demanding and intense a method, the stronger the immediate result but the lower the sustainability. For instance, hard rules on what and what not to eat and highly restrictive diets produce rapid weight loss. But they last only for a few days or weeks. Beyond that, most people are not able to continue to follow restrictions. You may have experienced this yourself if you have gone through a diet.

What we have also learnt is that for a method to be sustainable in the long term, it cannot be highly restrictive. It cannot revolve around rules to follow without us understanding the reasoning behind them.

This is why most diets and eating approaches don't stand the test of time. People who lose weight or improve their health by following diets tend to either quit or bounce around from one diet to another. This is because what really helped them get the results is following the rules and restrictions imposed by the diet. And for them to retain those results, they need to stick to that specific set of restrictions or find another set. But what they can't do without is restrictions.

This is why mindfulness matters when we eat. *Mindful eating is about being aware and taking control of what and how much you eat.* It is a skill. Not a set of restrictions. As with any skill, it requires practice. But once you acquire the skill, it will serve you for a long time.

A diet or a programme is like taking a cab to go from point A to point B. You have many cabs to choose from. You simply need to pick one, pay and jump in. It is quick and, if you don't fall off the wagon, you are guaranteed to get to point B. But mindful eating is like learning to drive. It takes longer. It requires patience. And you need to put in conscious work. But once you learn to drive, you have the ability to go from point A to point B whenever you want. And the ride doesn't end there. Once you get to point B, you can go on to point C and then D and continue your journey towards better health.

Mindful eating is the skill you need to master if you want to balance restriction and deprivation in the long term. Because mindfulness puts you in the driver's seat. It gives you control over your journey. It makes you independent.

> What do you prefer—diet or mindfulness? Which one do you think will serve you in the long term?

#11 Mindfulness begins with awareness

Do you know what you are eating? Do you know how much you are eating? Your immediate answers are probably yes and yes. But I urge you to take two minutes to think about it.

If you're eating naan, paneer curry and dal, are you conscious that you are eating wheat, oil, salt, vegetables, cheese, spices and lentils? Probably not. Most of us don't really think about what we eat. We see food, we make connections in our brain based on labels (food names) and past experiences, we eat and we move on. The act is done with very little thought. It is almost mindless.

Mindful eating is about being aware of what and how much food we need at any given instance and then making food choices based on that awareness.

The first and most important part of mindful eating is knowing what exactly we are eating. Ideally, every day, at every meal and every bite. This may sound like a complicated way of approaching food. But it is actually quite simple. You don't need to know the list of ingredients or the exact recipe of everything you eat. You simply need to take a moment and acknowledge what is on your plate. Try it. It will make sense almost immediately.

The second and an equally important part of mindful eating is knowing how much we are eating, especially in today's world of abundance. I'm not referring to calories, but to the quantity of food you're eating. Each person needs a certain quantity of food to stay healthy and in shape. This amount varies based on metabolism, which depends on genetics, body composition, body size and activity levels. There is no easy way to accurately tell the exact amount of energy and nutrients one needs. Neither is there is any need for that. Because the range for 'healthy' is quite wide.

And your body has an inbuilt mechanism to track energy levels and tell you when to eat and when to stop. As long as you make a conscious effort to be aware of what and how much you're eating, your body will take care of the balancing act.

> How mindful are you when you eat? Fully aware, completely clueless or somewhere in between? What do you think you should do to be more mindful

#12 Trust your body

Do you consciously control your calcium–magnesium balance? How about your blood pH? Cell volume? Respiration rate? How about the thousands of other bodily functions and processes? I'm sure you don't. In fact, you probably don't even know most of this happens. But somehow, for most people, for the most part, all these things are in control. Unless one does something specifically to affect these factors, these values are usually within the standard range. So we just let the body handle it.

Appetite regulation is also a function that the body is capable of handling rather well.

Say hello to ghrelin and leptin. They are hormones that help regulate appetite and feeding. Very simplistically, ghrelin is responsible for signalling hunger and leptin for signalling fullness. When there is no hormonal dysregulation, a normal person's body has very good control of these hormones and the function of appetite regulation. When the body is low on energy, ghrelin is secreted, you feel hungry, you seek food and eat. When you have eaten enough and there is sufficient energy in the body, leptin is secreted, you feel satiated and you stop eating. Simple enough.

Not really. Because the above process, which was a result of natural evolution, works perfectly only when the food being consumed is close to its natural state. Today, we rarely eat food like we used to before. We cook, process and engineer food to make it much more portable, shelf-stable and tasty. While this increases convenience, taste and pleasure, it also makes the energy inside the food more easily available to the body and packs more calories into each mouthful. All of this can be a good thing, but only if our metabolism and activity levels are high enough to make use of the extra energy. Unfortunately, that isn't the case today.

The mismatch between the fundamental need to consume more food and the modern need to restrict it occurs because our bodies are from the past but our brains are well into the future. Our brains want to experience all the delectable foods of today. But our bodies are not designed to tolerate them, especially given our current activity levels.

Clearly, this inbuilt mechanism to regulate appetite, though incredible, can't be relied on when eating modern foods. And so we need a smarter approach—one that takes advantage of both the inbuilt mechanism and our innate ability to use knowledge to modify behaviour.

> Before you turn the page to the next chapter, what do you think this smarter approach to regulating appetite is?

#13   The trick is to pay attention

People say that your body is always talking to you, and you need to listen to it. Obviously, your body is not literally 'talking' to you. But it is constantly sending you feedback in the form of signals. You can feel these signals. The only requirement is this: you need to pay attention.

One part of mindful eating is about paying attention to what we eat and how it makes us feel. The other part is using that information to make the right food choices. It does require practice, but it is not a hard skill to master. Because mindful eating is just about being smart when making food choices.

Making smart food choices doesn't mean eating only low-calorie foods or following a diet. It means understanding what you need from each meal and eating the foods that fulfil those needs. This will mean different things for different people. It will even mean different things for the same person at different times. For a professional athlete training multiple hours every day, energy-dense foods and a high-calorie diet are smart choices. But it isn't for someone who is trying to lose body weight. A cup of coffee is a smart choice for most people in the morning. It helps them be alert and active. But it may not be a smart choice for the same people at night because it might disrupt sleep.

In order to make the right food choices, you need to ask yourself a few simple questions every time you eat.

- What am I eating? Does it contain what I need from this meal, given my current goals?
- How much am I eating? Is this the right amount of food for me for this meal, given how hungry I am?
- If I eat this, how will I feel while eating? How will I feel right after? How will I feel after a few hours?

The act of asking yourself these questions to create awareness and making your food choices accordingly is what we call mindful eating.

The good thing about mindful eating is that you don't have to think too hard. You don't have to write anything down either. It is just an internal dialogue. By simply asking yourself these questions, you become aware of what is on your plate. This awareness will drive you towards making better, smarter choices as and when necessary. As simple as it is, the first few times may not be easy. You might forget or feel confused. But in a few days, this will become a simple but significant habit that guides you towards better food choices. And, hence, towards better health and fitness.

> Do you think you can spend 30 seconds before each meal to think about what you're eating? And do you think you can spend 30 seconds after each meal to think about how you're feeling? How about you try doing this during your next meal and see if it makes a difference?

#14 The only way to overcome 'food guilt'

Some foods are considered 'bad' in general. Trans-fats are an example. There may be a few more on that list, but 99 per cent of foods simply can't be categorised as just 'good' or 'bad'. Because the effect of a food varies depending on the person and situation.

We consider a food as good or bad based on how it serves us. We label it 'good' if it helps us get to our goals. We label it 'bad' if it takes us away from our goals. For instance, eating a kilo of spinach is 'good' if your goal is general health and weight management. It has plenty of fibre, is rich in vitamins A, C, K1 and B9, iron and calcium and is low in calories. But the same kilo of spinach can be 'bad' if your goal is to fuel rapidly right after running a marathon. It simply cannot provide you with what your body needs after intense exhaustion—quick energy and protein. A glass of a highly sweetened juice or a candy bar is 'bad' because it spikes blood sugar. But the same glass of juice or candy bar is 'good' because it can save someone with dangerously low blood sugar.

It is not the food itself that is good or bad. It is its *application* that counts—it could result in positive or negative outcomes based on how we use it. But does this distinction really matter? It does. Because viewing food as good or bad gives rise to strong emotions around it. We feel guilt when we eat 'bad' foods. And we feel pride when we eat 'good' foods.

We are emotional animals. Everything we do we do in order to feel a certain way. All of us have some form of a moral compass. We know we should do 'good things'. And not do—or at least try not to do—'bad things'. When we do good things, we pat ourselves on the back. We feel proud. When we do bad things, we are unhappy with ourselves. We feel guilt.

Chemically, our bodies are designed to increase the secretion of happy hormones when we do something we deem good, and decrease secretion when the opposite happens. So, when a food is deemed as good or bad, you end up feeling pride or guilt when you eat it. You just can't help it. And this feeling will determine your behaviour in the moments, and even days, that follow.

When you are trying to lose weight, cake is considered a 'bad' food choice. You too are aware of this. But the cake is very tempting, especially if you have been staying away from it. This causes an emotional battle in your brain. Should you eat it, feel good now and feel guilt afterwards? Or should you be strong, say no and feel pride later? At the end of this emotional battle, you will most certainly end up feeling one of the two.

Both pride and guilt are strong feelings that influence your subsequent actions. If you felt guilt, you may try to overcompensate for the cake with too much exercise or by skipping a meal. Or you might go on a downward spiral, claiming that you will never be able to stay consistent and you may as well call it quits. If you felt pride, you might pat yourself on the back for staying strong and move forward in your journey with your chin held high—until the next time you're at a similar crossroads.

But here is the thing—guilt and pride are two sides of the same coin. Where there is pride, there will be guilt. If one exists, the other exists too. In fact, they exist because of each other. So, if you really want to break this cycle of food guilt and pride that forces you to ride an emotional roller coaster, you need to be neutral and non-judgemental about food.

> How often have you let food related emotions dictate your actions? Think of a time when you overate or ate something that wasn't the best option and tried to compensate for that. Would you like to break that habit and view food differently?

#15 Experience food without judgement

You want to eat without guilt.

For that, you need to build a better relationship with food.

For that, you need to break the cycle of food guilt and pride.

For that, you need to stop viewing food as 'good' and 'bad'.

For that, you need a better way to relate to food.

And for that, you need a framework that is non-judgemental, outcome based and positive.

But first, what does food really provide us with? Energy and nutrients, yes. But what outcomes does food provide us with? You can name many but it comes down to these five—health, strength, comfort, luxury and fun.

Every time we eat, we do it to become healthier and grow stronger. But we also eat for taste—to feel comfortable, enjoy something luxurious and have fun. So, when we're eating a meal or a food item, the question is not whether it is good or bad, but which out of these five outcomes it serves.

Ideally, for us to eat in a manner that sustainably promotes well-being and be happy doing so, we need our meals to provide us with all five outcomes in the right balance. Saying no to comfort, luxury and fun leads to feeling deprived, and we won't be able to sustain that for more than a few weeks or months. This is what happens when you go on a diet. You eat 'clean' and be 'good'. But it is a matter of time before you give in to temptations, indulge in binge eating or quit the diet. That said, if we choose to prioritise comfort, luxury and fun over health and strength, well-being will certainly take a hit. This is usually the case when we eat guided only by taste and pleasure.

We need a balance. And if we can achieve that balance between these five outcomes, we can journey through life with happiness and well-being on our side and guilt and remorse out of the picture.

> If you could choose, how would you like to balance these five outcomes? Given your current goals, what would you prioritise and what would you de-prioritise?

#16 The practical nutrition framework

Whenever you see food, you analyse it. You may not even realise it. But you can't help yourself. It is this analysis that enables you to make instant food choices. Based on what your goals are at that time, you view food using different lenses to help you with this analysis.

Imagine yourself at a buffet with about thirty different food items. If your goal is mainly pleasure, you will use the 'tasty or not tasty' lens. If your goal is to eat only vegetarian food, you will use the 'veg or non-veg' lens. And if your goal is weight loss or health, you probably will use the 'good or bad' lens.

But, today, when you eat your next meal, I would like you to view food through a completely different lens. I call this the 'practical nutrition framework' and it goes like this:

- Whenever you see **vegetables** or **fruits**, think **health**.
- Whenever you see **protein**-rich foods, think **strength**.
- Whenever you see **starchy** foods, think **comfort**.
- Whenever you see **fatty** foods, think **luxury**.
- Whenever you see **sweet** foods, think **fun**.

Vegetables and fruits are health foods. You need a lot of these because they are rich in water, fibre, vitamins and minerals and scarce in calories. They are perfect for anyone looking to improve health without gaining extra weight. So, your goal should be to get at least two servings of vegetables each day and, if possible, three to five servings of vegetables and fruits combined. (1 serving = 1 cup = 240 ml)

Protein-rich foods = strength. Eating sufficient protein will enable growth and strength—it will build bones and muscles, provide structural support at the cellular level and improve immunity. Depending on our goals, we need about 0.8–2.5 grams of protein for every kilo of our body weight. While the current protein recommendation is 0.8 grams for every kilo of your body weight, that is simply meant to prevent a deficiency. And that means, it is the absolute bare minimum you need. Ideally, here is how much protein you need:

1–1.25 g/kg of body weight	General health and deficiency prevention with no fitness focus
1.25–1.75 g/kg of body weight	Fitness improvement and weight loss
1.75–2.5 g/kg of body weight	Muscle building, extreme calorie deficit for bodybuilding

Starch is comfort. Because starchy foods like rice, roti, pasta, poha, idli, dosa, potatoes, etc. provide us with not much micronutrients or fibre, but with a warm and fuzzy feeling of comfort. This is true especially for us Indians who are used to eating a carb-dominant diet.

Fat is a luxury. Because fat adds richness and enhances flavour. But fat is also the most calorie-dense macronutrient—9 kcal per gram vs 4 kcal per gram for protein and carbohydrates. For this reason, not everyone can afford to eat too much fat, and considering it a luxury will help you make smart choices around them.

As for sweet foods, we don't eat them for health or for energy, but to feel pleasure and to add excitement to our meals. Think of them as fun, and enjoy them in moderation.

Why is this framework important? Because all foods have a purpose. Some are meant to nourish us physically while some others are meant to aid us mentally and emotionally. But it is completely up to us to define the outcomes and find balance. And 'the practical nutrition framework' can help you make smart food choices irrespective of who you are, what you're eating, when you're eating and where you're eating it.

> Close your eyes and envision this framework for a second. Are you able to view your meals in terms of health, strength, comfort, luxury and fun? Based on your current goals, how much of each do you think you need in your life?

#17 Health, strength, comfort, luxury and fun

By now, the larger picture of the practical nutrition framework and its use should be clear to you. But we need to go a level deeper and understand which foods fall under each of these five categories.

What qualifies as health? Vegetables and fruits, and it is important not to get lost in the specifics. Given that we are working on taking control of nutrition in the long term, our focus needs to be on the big picture. So, any and all vegetables qualify, except potatoes and corn. Potatoes because they contain mostly starch. And corn because it is a grain (maize) and not a vegetable. The only exception with fruit is avocado because it is rich in fat. It is certainly a healthy choice. But it's high in fat and consequently dense in calories.

What qualifies as strength? Any and all foods that are rich in protein. So, meat, seafood, eggs, protein supplements, cheese (including paneer), tofu, tempeh and soya chunks belong here. If none of these are an option for you, milk, curd, lentils and beans can take their place. But do keep in mind that these are not our first preference because they are not too rich in protein and come with quite a bit of carbohydrates or fat compared with the first list.

What about comfort? Any and all foods that are rich in starch. So, rice, roti, idli, dosa, parantha, naan, kulcha, poha, pasta, idiyappam, potatoes, corn, quinoa, couscous and pretty much every other grain-based food item will belong here.

How about luxury? Any food item that contains a lot of fat. So, oil, cream, mayonnaise, ghee, butter, nuts and all other high-fat foods belong here. But remember that prepared foods and dishes that are oily, creamy, fried or rich also belong here. Butter chicken, dal makhani, malai kofta and anything fried are all examples of such food.

And fun? Well, anything that adds sweetness to a food and any food that is sweet. And that means sugar, honey, jaggery and other sweeteners and sweet foods that are made using these. One thing to keep in mind here is that while fruit falls under health, dried fruit and fruit juice will fall under fun. This is because when the water is removed from fruits, they become essentially nature's little bullets of sugar. And fruit juice is like eating fruit without chewing, which means we're likely to consume a lot more sugar than when eating fruit.

The specific micronutrient content and macronutrient splits may vary, but don't let yourself get lost in the details. Instead, simplify, understand the big picture and work on choosing wisely.

> Think about all the foods you eat on a daily basis. Are you able to categorise them? What category do each of them fall under?

#18 Mindless eating—the guaranteed way to ill health

When you build a meal based only on taste, chances are it is highly comforting, luxurious, moderately fun, but it barely promotes health or strength. In nutritional terms, the meal will most probably be high in starch and fat, contain a good amount of sugar and will have minimal protein and vegetables.

Think about what most people order when they go to a restaurant—garlic naan with paneer or chicken tikka masala, some dal makhani and ice cream or gulab jamun (or both!). Rich, fun and certainly delicious. Same deal with biryani, raita and shahi tukda. Or pizza, garlic bread and cola. Even a seemingly simple meal of steamed jasmine rice, Thai green curry and coconut custard is rich in fat and starch, moderately high in sugar and contains hardly any protein or fibre.

We naturally gravitate towards such meals because we are hardwired to seek pleasure and reward. And meals that are highly comforting, luxurious and fun provide that pleasure by stimulating the reward system in our body. Why? Because all these foods are dense in energy. And our body, which is still living in a time of potential food scarcity, craves them because of how much energy they provide and how quickly they provide it.

This, in a nutshell, is why you end up gaining weight and developing chronic diseases when you eat mindlessly. When you don't apply your mind and consciously restrict yourself, your body has nothing stopping it from seeking out these high-density foods that release happiness hormones, which make you feel joy and pleasure.

Our way of controlling this behaviour today is through diets, discipline and programmes. But they only work in the short term. The simplest and most efficient way to combat the potential ill-effects of mindless eating in the long term is through mindful eating.

> If you had no weight or health concerns and could eat whatever you wanted, what would you order at a restaurant? Is it geared towards health and strength or towards comfort, luxury and fun?

#19 Start by building a smart plate of food

Smart eating begins with building a smart plate of food. So we're going to build your plate together. And we're going to build it conceptually so you can apply this framework to any meal—whenever you eat it, wherever you eat it and whoever you eat it with.

Imagine yourself getting ready for a meal. You have your plate, and there is food in front of you. Or you're at a restaurant, and you have the menu card in your hands.

The first thing you need to do is to look for *'health'*. Based on where you are and what is available, what are your options in this category? Can you spot all the vegetables and fruits available? Great. Now, fill a third to half of your plate with vegetables and fruits. Some days you'll have plenty to choose from. And some days your only options might be onions and tomatoes. It doesn't matter. Keep it simple. Pick out the best options from whatever is available.

The next thing you need to do is to look for *'strength'*. Protein—the one macronutrient that you're not getting enough of and is not easy to find. Look hard and find what is available. Fill a third of your plate with protein-rich foods. You may have top-level options like seafood, meat, eggs, cheese and tofu. Or you may only have mid-level options like curd, milk and beans. Again, try and make the best out of what you have. Note that 'fatty protein' may be part of the menu. Examples are fried fish, Chicken 65, paneer fingers, seafood in a rich and creamy gravy. When that happens, try to pick out the protein from the fat (like scooping out the meat from a gravy). If it's too weird (like scraping the breading off fried chicken), don't do it. Eat it as is or skip it. Keep it simple. Always.

At this point, your plate should be two-thirds to three-fourths full with plenty of protein and vegetables. If it is, that's awesome. You have already built a plate that is loaded with health and strength. You have set yourself up for success.

If you're happy with just this and don't think you will feel deprived, you're done building your plate. This is your meal and it has everything you 'need'. But maybe not everything you want. And you may not be happy with a plate like this for every meal. But remember that a meal focusing on just health and strength will contain everything you need to function well physically. Because protein-rich foods typically come with some fat and vegetables and fruits contain enough starch and sugar in addition to fibre and micronutrients.

If health and strength don't cut it for you (as for most people), it's now time to seek 'comfort'. Starchy foods are what you need, and you need just enough of them. Too little and you may feel deprived. Too much and you get lethargic. In a typical home or restaurant, you will find plenty of comfort options. Don't eat all of them. Instead, pick the one that will serve the purpose and fill whatever little space is left on your plate with it.

Don't panic. I'm not suggesting that you do 'low carb' or 'keto'. This is called starch regulation. Let me explain.

The most abundantly consumed macronutrient today is carbohydrates, mostly in the form of starches such as rice and bread. Given how susceptible we are to chronic metabolic diseases and weight gain, we need to regulate our starch consumption. But regulation is different from just reduction. While reduction might be a part of regulation, how much you can consume depends on your current health and activity levels. Starch is not bad. But starchy foods contain mostly energy, with hardly any nutrients. So, unless your activity levels are very high, you don't need too much carbohydrate. In short, eat more starch if you're highly active. Eat less starch if you're not.

Now, back to your plate. What do you see?

- A third to half of your plate filled with vegetables and fruits
- A third filled with protein-rich foods
- A third to a quarter with starchy foods.

Excellent. You have built yourself a meal that promotes health and strength and is reasonably comforting. You would think this is perfect. But, most people on most occasions, be it a special birthday or random Tuesday, will seek luxury and fun.

When it comes to *luxury* (fat), you don't really need to seek and add. The process of cooking food involves fat to make food tasty, rich and flavourful. So, chances are your plate is already luxurious enough.

If your goal is weight loss or cardiovascular health, luxury isn't something you can afford. You need to ensure it is on the lower end—avoid foods that are oily, fried, creamy or rich. If you're not concerned about your weight and are in great health, you can increase this a little. Maybe add some ghee to your rice. Or some gravy to your protein. But, no matter who you are, too much luxury will hurt you. Especially when clubbed with comfort and fun. In nutritional terms, a diet that is consistently high in fat, carbohydrates and sugar is always detrimental to health. So, be mindful of your choices and be reasonable with your portions, even if you're in supreme health.

And that leaves us with *fun*—sweet foods. But first, take a moment to think. Why are you seeking sweet foods? Definitely not for hunger or health. You probably just want to finish your meal with something fun. And you can certainly do that. It just comes down to how much. Too little fun is boring. And too much fun is spoiling. So, what's the right amount of fun?

Depending on what your goals are, it can range from 'as little as possible' to 'as much as necessary'.

- If you're diabetic or insulin resistant, 'as little as possible' should mean 'nothing'. Ideally, you should have a piece of fruit and end your meal.
- If you're in good health but are working on weight loss, 'as much as necessary' means 'as little as possible'. Start with a tiny amount. Say, one teaspoon. Eat it and see how you feel. Give it a minute. If you really need another teaspoon, go for it. Repeat the process. In two to four teaspoons, you will feel surprisingly satisfied and won't find a reason to eat more. This is especially true if you have had plenty of protein and vegetables in your meal.
- If you don't have any health or weight problems and are active, you can afford to have a little more fun. But I'd still recommend that you do the above and find your optimal quantity. Because that's how you can continue to not have any health or weight problems.

And there you go. Your ideal meal is here. One that provides you with plenty of health and strength, just enough comfort, affordable luxury and a little dose of fun. Another example of 'simple, not easy', but if you can use the practical nutrition framework consistently, nutrition will cease to be confusing or complicated and eating will become a simple, intuitive and joyful experience.

> Visualise your next meal. Using the practical nutrition framework to guide you, what choices would you make? What do you think your plate would look like?

#20 Food quantity matters

Let's talk about finance and wealth management for a second.

Most people do something to earn money. We call the thing they do 'work' and the money they make 'a salary' or 'profit'. This is unavoidable, because everyone needs money to live. But who among all these people should think about managing their money? You know, things like saving money, making smart investments and planning for the future? Only the rich? Or, because the rich are already rich, only the poor? Of course not. Managing finances and wealth with a goal of a safer and more comfortable future is for everyone.

Weight and health management are the same. Irrespective of who you are and what you do, you need health and mobility to live a comfortable life. Maintaining your weight in an optimal range, working on your ability to move and living a pain-free life make up a big part of it. You don't have to be skinny or ripped to live your best life. But you can't argue that being obese, in pain or diseased will severely affect your quality of life.

What you eat determines your health, and how much you eat determines your body weight and body size. But if you eat too much of the healthy stuff, there will be unhealthy consequences. This is why food quantity matters. Weight loss need not be a concern or goal for everyone. But weight management is certainly something everyone needs to work on. Because, like everything else in nature, optimal applies here too.

Just like how managing your everyday finances well will help you with wealth management and financial freedom, managing your everyday fitness and weight will help you with health management and physical freedom.

In the very long term, it is this health and physical freedom that will allow you to take advantage of the time, wealth and financial freedom that you will have earned through decades of hard work. It will help you move without pain, explore the world, do activities you enjoy doing and, most importantly, not be a burden to anyone else.

> How has your body weight changed over the last three years? How would you like to manage it over the next ten years?

#21 Eat as well as you can, but only as much as necessary

Food quality will determine your health. Food quantity will determine your body weight. Together, they will determine your body composition.

Mindful eating and the practical nutrition framework will guide you sufficiently on food quality but only to a certain extent when it comes to food quantity. 'How much should I eat?' still remains to be answered.

Over the years, we have come up with many methods to answer this question. Calorie counting, portion control, food group elimination and intermittent fasting are four different ways to control the quantity of food that we consume. They all work in the short term. But in the long term, they all fall apart. Calorie counting is not accurate. Portion control (weighing and measuring) is too complicated to sustain for the regular person. Food group elimination works until people figure out loopholes (keto cookies, anyone?). Intermittent fasting gradually becomes a case of people eating bigger meals in a smaller time window. Somehow, we always figure out how to eat more calories than we should.

Why does this happen? Because our bodies don't really want us to lose weight. As annoying as it may seem, this is a survival tactic. And it is meant to keep us away from malnutrition and starvation.

When we eat fewer calories than necessary, the body immediately responds by downregulating our metabolism. In other words, when energy inflow is reduced, the body reduces energy outflow and tries to establish homeostasis—a state of balance that is necessary for health, functionality and survival.

But restricting food quantity and, hence, calories is important. Because a consistent calorie surplus could result in unintended weight gain and the accompanying health issues. For instance, a calorie surplus of just 200 calories per day can result in a weight gain of up to 20 kilos in two years!

Unfortunately, however, we're now left with four unreliable ways to control food quantity. Luckily, our bodies have a preprogrammed way of regulating food quantity and energy inflow based on need. This is called satiety.

> Before we started thinking in calories, how do you think people measured food? How did they know how much to eat? Do you think food metrics and recommendations in the form of portion sizes and calories have stunted our ability to listen to our bodies and eat accordingly?

#22 Satisfied or stuffed?

Why do you stop eating?

You start eating a meal. And at some point, you stop eating. Why and when does that happen? Is it when you finish your plate? When you feel full? When you literally can't stuff in another bite? Maybe all of these are right answers at different points of time. But, most often, we eat till we finish our plates or till we actually feel full. This is a problem, and I'll explain why.

'Finish your plate' is something most of us were told as kids. Add to this the unavoidable *'so many kids don't have any food'*, and there is no way we can choose to not finish our plates. And till today, we have this habit of finishing our plates. This *may* be a good thing from the perspective of reducing food wastage, but from an energy regulation perspective, it's not. Because it means we're eating as much as is served and not as much as we need. Similarly, stopping after you feel full isn't helping either. Because feeling full means you've already eaten more than you need.

The only way to regulate energy inflow and sustain it in the long term is to understand 'satiety' and practise it regularly in every meal. *Satiety is the feeling of being physically and psychologically satisfied after consuming food.* And this is different from feeling 'full' or 'stuffed'.

Usually, this is how the hunger–satiety scale goes:

Extremely hungry	I'm starving, I can eat a horse!
Very hungry	I can't wait to eat!
Hungry	OK, I'm ready to eat.
Satisfied	**I'm happy. I'm not full but I'm good for the next few hours.**
Full	I think I ate more than I should have.
Stuffed	Oh boy, I can't breathe!

If you're thinking 'All of this is based on feel and not on hard metrics. How am I to figure out exactly how much I should eat?', you're absolutely right. But 'feeling satisfied' is actually a very memorable and comfortable feeling that you'll learn to identify as soon as you start eating mindfully.

And about the 'don't waste food' situation—here is a solution. If you serve yourself more than you need, eat only what you need and save the rest for later. Or, if that's not possible, throw it away. But don't throw it into your body. Because overeating for the sake of it is the worst reason to overeat. The smart thing to do is to learn from this experience. Next time, serve yourself smaller portions and scale up till you have had enough. This way you won't find yourself in a situation where you need to waste food again. And about the people who don't have food—there are hundreds of ways to make a difference. But I can guarantee you that you eating more food than you need is not one of them.

> Think back to your last meal. Did you end the meal feeling satisfied, full or stuffed? How much food do you think it takes to go from satisfied to stuffed?

#23 Knowing when to stop is a skill

You have your keys in your hand. And about four feet in front of you is a single-seater sofa. You want to throw your keys on the sofa. You swing the arm holding the keys back. You pause. As you swing it forward, you let go of the keys. They fly in the air and land on the sofa. You walk away like that was nothing and move on to your next task.

Most people would take this shot and get it right. No problem. But you can't deny the fact that this is a skill. Your brain, in a split second, did some complicated computations to make this simple shot happen—it figured out how far you needed to swing your arm back, at what force you had to swing it forward, at what point and how much the elbow had to bend, when the wrist had to come into play, when the keys had to be released. And all this based on an estimate of how much the set of keys weighs.

This process too lacks hard metrics. This too is completely based on 'feel'. You probably won't be able to do this computation on a piece of paper if I asked you to. But you did it in your head. It's amazing how incredible our brains are.

Knowing how much food and energy you need is also a skill. Your body can learn and become better at it if you work with it. No hard metrics here too and it's impossible to compute on paper for the layperson. But satiety is easily learnt through practice. Like any skill, all of us are capable of this to varying extents. Some of us tend to pick up these signals easily. Some others struggle with it, especially if there is any hormonal dysfunction or imbalance with ghrelin (hunger hormone) and leptin (satiety hormone). But irrespective of what our potential is, all of us can improve with practice.

And practically, practice means that every time you eat, you need to:

- be aware of what and how much you're eating
- pay attention to how you're feeling
- eat till you're satisfied and not till you're full
- make a conscious effort to learn from each meal.

Sounds like a lot. But you already do this process of doing–learning–doing better–learning more–doing even better without your knowledge in many fundamental aspects of your life. Examples include walking, bathing, brushing, driving, writing and much more. It doesn't take a lot of time or mental energy. It just requires you to remember to do it. And within a week or two of practice, you'll be able to differentiate between how much food satisfies you and how much food makes you feel full and know exactly when to stop eating.

> Talking about innate skills, how good a singer are you? How do you handle spice compared with others? How quickly do you understand directions or solve puzzles? What are some of your skills that you take for granted? If you practised those skills with the goal of improving, do you think you would get better at them?

#24 The faster you eat, the more you eat

Two simple and seemingly harmless behaviours can make appetite regulation hard—eating speed and eating frequency.

You may have noticed that the hungrier you are, the faster you eat. And the faster you eat, the less awareness and control you have over how much you eat. This is normal, and again, a survival mechanism. When your stomach is empty, ghrelin is released. Hunger is signalled, and you feel uncomfortable. If you don't attend to it, the level of hunger and discomfort increases. The body gets into a slight panic mode, and the brain focuses most of its attention on seeking energy. This is why any and all food, or even images of food, appear tasty when you're very hungry. Once food is available, in the absence of conscious thought and effort, we consume it as quickly as possible because we want ghrelin levels to drop and the feeling of hunger to stop. We want to go back to being comfortable.

This behaviour is normal. But the concern is overeating. When you're ravenously hungry and wolfing down whatever is on your plate, you taste the food less. You're not sure what each bite actually contains. Your rate of food consumption per minute is high. And you don't really track how much food you've eaten.

Also, when you eat in this manner, it feels just great for the first few minutes. But in a little while, almost suddenly, you feel full. And based on how fast and how much you ate, your situation could be anything from 'That was good, I'm full!' to 'Oh man, I feel like there is a rock inside my stomach!'

The reason for this is that there is a small lag between a few processes in our bodies. And this lag is responsible for a lot of the overeating we do.

> The next time you're hungry, observe yourself. Are you calm and patient or are you in a hurry to get food in? Do regular foods appear more delicious than usual? How hard is it for you to make the right food choices?

#25 Slow down

The body has a whole appetite regulation system with fancy hormones and flashy receptors. But does it all break down if you eat fast? To be honest, yes. We are far from being perfect.

Truth is, it takes about 20 minutes for the brain to understand if we are satiated and suppress appetite accordingly. Why does this happen? Remember, satiety is a physical and psychological feeling of satisfaction. There's a lot going on here. To suppress appetite, your brain relies on information from taste and smell receptors and nerve cells on your stomach lining, which sense stretching, and hormones like ghrelin, leptin, PPY, GLP 1 and insulin. While electrical signals through nerve cells are transmitted instantaneously, hormones need to travel through blood. That takes a while.

The kind of foods you eat also determines how quickly these signals are sent to your brain. Foods that are rich in fibre tend to suppress ghrelin, stimulate appetite-suppressing hormones and also apply pressure on the stomach's stretch receptors more than processed foods. It is for the same reason, calorie for calorie, foods that are high in volume but low in energy (like fruits, vegetables and popped corn) make you feel fuller sooner than foods that are low in volume but high in energy (like oil, nuts, fried food and dried fruit).

The logical way to address this is to make smart food choices, which we covered in detail earlier. But also to give your brain the time it needs. You need to eat slowly so that your brain can catch up and update you on your satiety levels before you overeat. A very simple concept, but one that proves to be quite hard to execute.

In the list of 'harder than you think' things to do, slow eating will rank right up there. Anyone who has tried eating slowly for the first time will quickly realise that eating for twenty minutes is no easy task! It's true. It takes more than just slowing down to slow down.

Most of us would find it very hard to get past ten minutes when we eat a reasonable amount of food. Some of us might struggle to make it to even five. But we can extend it further by following these simple guidelines:

- *Take smaller bites.* They don't have to be tiny. Just make sure you're not taking in large mouthfuls.
- *Chew every bite thoroughly.* Roughly twenty to forty times, based on the texture of what you're eating.
- *Keep your hands idle when chewing.* And that means don't prepare your next bite while you're still chewing this one.
- *Pause between bites.* Consider eating as an interval-based process and not a continuous one. So, take a bite, chew, swallow, pause to take a breath, prepare the next bite, take the bite, chew and so on, as opposed to taking a mouthful, preparing your next mouthful while chewing, swallowing and getting the next mouthful in immediately.

This requires conscious thought and a bit of practice, but it is a habit that, once built, will last for a long time.

> How long do you think it takes you to eat a plate of food today? If you consciously slowed down, how long do you think you could last?

#26 The more often you eat, the more mistakes you make

If there is a problem, we want it to be solved. Or we want to solve it ourselves. And the person or company who solves it best or better than the rest makes money. It's business and it's fair.

Snacking is a big problem. So snacking is big business. But is this problem even worth solving?

The snacking industry is huge, to say the least. There are literally thousands of options. Some tasty, some healthy, some tasty and healthy. But let me ask you this—why do you need a snack?

Animals need a constant supply of energy and nutrients. But we humans don't need to consume them constantly. Our bodies have learnt and evolved the ability to digest food, extract energy and nutrients quickly, store them and then release them over a period of time based on need. This incredible ability is what allows us to do cool things like building cities, going to space and creating art instead of spending half of our days eating and chewing our food like cows do.

Most of us eat three meals a day—breakfast, lunch and dinner. A snack is essentially a bridge between any two meals. Its only purpose is to keep hunger away for an hour or two and prevent us from getting too hungry and uncomfortable before the next meal.

But since the snacking industry is huge, snacks have become very creative. Today, snacks are not here just to address nutrition and hunger, but also taste, boredom and experience. We snack not only when we're hungry but also when we're bored. When we want something yummy. When we meet someone. And even when we just want to take a break from our day.

But the truth remains that the more often we eat, the more often we need to make smart food choices and control ourselves from overeating. So, unless extremely disciplined, a snacking habit is only making things harder from a health and weight management perspective.

And hence, my recommendations with respect to snacking are the following:

- *If possible, kick the habit. Don't snack.* This is a big change for some but certainly possible. By eating nutritious satiating meals rich in protein and vegetables and by spacing your meals out such that no two meals are more than five or six hours apart. For example, breakfast at nine, lunch at two and dinner at eight is a much simpler structure to handle than breakfast at eight, lunch at twelve and dinner at nine.
- *If you have to snack, stick to a small portion of protein and vegetables or fruit.* Any simple protein like eggs, cheese, curd or milk and any vegetable (even leftovers from the previous meal) or fruit will work. Keep it simple. And yes, that means coffee and chai are OK but samosas, cutlets, chips and cookies can't become regulars.

What about protein bars? Digestive biscuits? Sugar-free laddus? The list of options is endless. If your goal with snacking is fun or pleasure, many options will fit the bill. But if your overall goal is health and a snack is just a way to get you through to dinner, keep it simple and work on kicking the habit. Because *the fact is a snack is a meal we don't need.*

> Do you snack? When do you usually snack? Do you really need that snack? How can you get more protein and vegetables in your meals and space them out better?

#27 It doesn't matter when

Why, what, how much and when are the four questions that help us address nutrition effectively. While the first three are very important, *when* you're eating something doesn't carry the same importance for the everyday person looking to improve health and fitness.

To put it very simply, unless you are some kind of athlete looking to achieve peak performance and need to compete to a point where every second, inch or gram matters, meal frequency and meal timing don't matter as much. As long as you're consuming the required amount of energy, macro- and micronutrients in a day, it matters less when and in how many meals you're consuming them.

Nutrient timing does have an effect on the performance of the human body. But practically, nutrient consistency will have a larger impact than nutrient timing. If you are someone who prefers eating small meals throughout the day and if it works for you, that is a great fit. But if you are someone who likes eating big meals and are OK eating infrequently, this is a great fit. The goal is to find the eating pattern that allows you to eat everything you need to eat and be sustainable in the long term. Because, if you can zoom out for a bit, health and fitness are more about acquiring and utilising nutrients consistently over a long period of time than about timing things perfectly for a short period.

This also means, from a weight loss perspective, it doesn't matter when you eat your carbohydrates and how big each meal is. As long as you are within your total caloric limit and are consuming the macro- and micronutrients you need, a deficit will be created and you will lose weight.

All this said, here are a few things you need to keep in mind:

- *Eat as many meals as is right for you.* But don't go to extremes on either side. Two to five meals are great, but one is too few and six or more is usually too many.
- *Eat protein around the time you train.* No reason to be watching the clock closely and chugging protein shakes minutes after training. But make sure there is some protein in your system before and after training. This is meant as a safety protocol to minimise muscle protein breakdown during intense activity and help with recovery.
- *Avoid eating huge meals close to bedtime.* This is not because that food will be converted to fat when you sleep. It is simply to make sure your sleep is not affected by the digestive process.

Theoretically, there are benefits to eating certain foods at certain times during the day. But practically, there is enough research to prove that every eating pattern is only effective if the consumer is consistent. This is why convenience that leads to consistency matters more than anything else.

> How many meals do you currently eat? Do you think this number can or should be reduced or increased? Or would you rather change what you are eating at each meal?

#28 The incredible Indian diet

Many hundreds of years ago, there was a school in a village. And right outside it lived a cat. Every morning, as soon as the kids assembled and school was about to start, the cat would show up and meow, asking for food. The teachers and students realised that the only way to stop the cat from meowing was to feed the cat. So they fed the cat. The cat shut up. And they started school. The cat made a habit out of this and the practice of feeding a cat continued for so long that it became a tradition.

Many years passed and the school was shut down. A few decades later, the school was reopened. The villagers gathered to watch their kids attend their first day in the new school. Just as school was about to start, one of the kids' parents stood up and said, 'We need to feed the cat before we start school.' And the teacher said, 'Which cat?' The parent said, 'It is tradition to feed *a* cat before we start school and so it needs to be done.' But there was no cat. So, the villagers found a cat, brought the cat to school, fed the cat and then started school. Everyone was happy and the tradition continued.

Sometimes, traditions are solutions to problems that don't exist anymore. They may have once been perfect solutions and may have served us greatly. But, with time, they don't serve the same purpose. They need to evolve. Without evolving, they stop being relevant solutions and continue living on as one of those things that 'we need to do because that's how we have always done it'.

The carbohydrate-dominant Indian diet is an example. If we do a complete macronutrient breakdown of a typical Indian meal, we will learn that it contains mostly carbohydrates, with moderate amounts of fat and minimal protein and vegetables. But there was a reason for this.

Back in the day, life was much less comfortable and much more active. And so, our dietary requirements and food systems were quite different. First, we needed much more energy on a daily basis to be able to complete all the work (mostly physical) we had to. This was necessary just to maintain one's body weight. Because everything required movement. From sourcing water to doing daily chores to cooking to working to visiting, everything involved, or rather demanded, movement.

Second, energy was not as easy to procure. Food storage and increasing shelf life was not as simple a deal as it is today. Commercial refrigeration was not invented till the 1850s, and the household fridges we take for granted today weren't available till about a hundred years ago.

And third, since we had to consume more energy on a daily basis, we used grains and other calorie dense (but nutrient scarce) foods as vehicles to transport the required nutrients to the body. This is why every Indian meal contains a starchy food item along with which protein and vegetables are consumed.

So back then, eating a lot of rice or roti or other starch-dominant foods and making them the centre of the meal made perfect sense. This way, we got the calories we needed and we were able to get in the required nutrients from the sides, which were typically vegetables and/or meat. But today, this way of eating doesn't serve us the same way. Because it is a solution for a problem that doesn't exist anymore.

Today's problem is that our bodies experience an abundance of energy and a scarcity of nutrients. We are overfed but undernourished. The solution to this problem is what we've been discussing all along—mindful eating aimed at balancing energy and nutrients.

This does NOT mean that Indian food is unhealthy. In fact, Indian food, with its innumerable vegetable-based dishes, health-promoting spices and millions of traditional yet easily modifiable recipes, has the potential to be one of the healthiest ways of eating. The only thing—we need to evolve. We need to address the problem we are facing today instead of addressing the problem we were facing hundreds of years ago. And, practically, that just means eating more protein and vegetables and less starch and sugar. Simple, not easy. Wouldn't you agree?

> How often do you eat traditional Indian food in your house? Is it mostly 'comfort' with a side of 'health' and 'strength'? How can you turn this around?

#29 If it is homemade, it is healthy

Well, not really.

First, it is important to differentiate between health and hygiene. Hygiene is about preventing infections through cleanliness. Health is about promoting well-being through nutrients. Home food can certainly be more hygienic than food from a store or a restaurant. This is because kitchens in homes are usually cleaner and ingredients are handled more cautiously. This will indeed help us with general safety and prevent us from picking up infections and food-borne illnesses. But how health-promoting a food is depends on the ingredients and the quality and quantity of each ingredient rather than on where it is cooked.

Typically, pizza is not considered health-promoting but a salad is. This is because when I say 'pizza', you're imagining a decadent one loaded with cheese and all your favourite toppings. And when I say salad, you're imagining a bowl of simple vegetables with a light dressing. But technically, a pizza can be made to be health-promoting and a salad can be the absolute opposite. How about a thin-crust pizza with a tomato sauce base, low-fat high protein mozzarella cheese loaded with grilled chicken and vegetables? And how about a salad that contains plenty of dried fruit and fried protein and is doused in a deliciously creamy dressing?

The deal with home food is the same. If the choice of ingredients is right and they are high in quality and optimal in quantity, home food is absolutely health promoting. But if it is the opposite, then it doesn't matter in which kitchen it is cooked and who cooked it with how much love—the food will not be health promoting.

Take, for instance, a plate of homemade biryani cooked with plenty of meat and just enough fresh oil. Compare it with a biryani that you order off the street. Which one is more health promoting? The homemade one, of course. Why? Not because it was made at home but because it has a better nutrient split and fresh cooking oil compared with what you may get on the street or in a restaurant. Now, compare a plate of poached eggs, toast and a side of sauteed vegetables ordered in from a restaurant against a homemade meal of poori and chole. Which one is more health promoting? The eggs, toast and vegetables meal. Though cooked outside, it contains ingredients that are more health promoting and is cooked using methods that are more health promoting.

So, while home food has a safe and comforting feel to it, do remember that health is less about where a meal is being cooked and more about what is being used, how much of it is being used and how it is being cooked.

> How often do you eat out or order in? More importantly, what do you order? How can you make your meals high on 'health' and 'strength' irrespective of where they are cooked?

#30 Use, don't abuse

Prevention is better than cure. And it certainly helps to focus on prevention from as early as possible. But if there is a dysfunction or a disease, a cure is needed. And the focus absolutely needs to be on curing the dysfunction there is today and on preventing future dysfunctions.

Good nutrition can help you stay healthy, strengthen your immune system and prevent metabolic diseases. But health is such a wide and deep phenomenon that is affected by a multitude of factors that even your best efforts might not be able to keep you in perfect health. Because not everything is under your control. While you can control what you eat, how active you are and how well you sleep, you still don't have control over your genetic make-up and predispositions, the environment and pollutants around you, the quality of the food available to you and the infections you may pick up from the millions of microbes coexisting with you.

So, in spite of making the effort, a good percentage of people, especially after a certain age, find themselves dealing with deficiencies and diseases. This could be a result of suboptimal lifestyles from the past or because of the many uncontrollables. In any case, these deficiencies and diseases need to be addressed to lead active, comfortable and happy lives.

This is exactly why we have a healthcare system. And, as imperfect as it may be, this system can help us address deficiencies through supplements when they can't be addressed through lifestyle change and cure diseases using medical interventions when one's condition has gone beyond what is treatable with nutrition and lifestyle improvements. *The important thing to keep in mind both with respect to supplements and medicines is that it is absolutely OK to use them, but it is definitely not OK to abuse them.* This simply means that you need to take supplements and medicines only if and when you really need them.

You need supplementation only when you are deficient in something and are unable to get it sustainably through natural meals. Not because a celebrity is endorsing it. Or because everyone is taking it. Or because the company used attractive words in their marketing campaigns. This applies to every supplement, be it as general as protein, vitamin D and magnesium, or as specific as carnitine, citrulline and beta-alanine. And the only way to do this correctly is to talk to a doctor, do the necessary tests to understand what you are deficient in and then start supplementing.

And when it comes to medication, it just comes down to being sensible. Remember, medicines are not meant to be shortcuts to health. They are powerful substances that can help when done right and hurt when done wrong. So, always, talk to a doctor before taking medicines, don't overmedicate and please don't build a pill-popping habit.

If you are someone who has a health condition or a deficiency, lifestyle changes are a great idea to improve your health. But please make sure you talk to your doctor before you make any changes, especially if you are currently on medication. Your doctor, who should be made aware of your current health and future goals, will view all the different parameters of your health and provide their expert opinion, which (hopefully) will be a combination of lifestyle changes, supplementation and medication.

> Have you ever wondered if taking a supplement can improve your health drastically? Are you ready to test and understand the nature and extent of your deficiencies before supplementing?

#31 Simplicity presents itself before and after complexity

We start with simplicity because we don't know better and we end with simplicity because we now know better.

Some things *are* complicated. Anything *can be made* complicated. But almost everything can be simplified if you understand the first principles. And nutrition is definitely one of those things that can be simplified. So, when things are not under your control, when you're not sure of what choices to make, when you're travelling, when you're busy at work, when you're feeling low and don't have the mental energy to think much about your meals, simplify your meals using this one line:

Eat protein, vegetables and starch in every meal, and don't overeat.

That's it.

That's literally it.

Irrespective of what your goals are, where you are, which meal of the day it is and what is available, eat protein, vegetables and starch in every meal and eat only to satiety or below satiety. For some meals, you may get more protein and vegetables, and for some you'll get mostly carbohydrates. That's OK. Don't complicate it. Because every meal is an opportunity to nourish your body with nutrients and improve our health. With about a hundred meals every month and more than a thousand meals every year, you will get plenty of opportunities to build long-term health and fitness through nutrition. And this simple base of protein, vegetables, starch and satiety will lend itself as a solid foundation for you to build on.

When in doubt, simplify.

> Do you have a better understanding of nutrition now? Are you able to zoom out, view things from a macro scale and simplify what good nutrition means for you in your life?

SECTION 3

MOVEMENT

#32   Movement is mandatory

Deep in the jungle, a lion wakes up. And many hundreds of yards away, so does a gazelle. The lion is a predator. Afraid of no animal, hunts at will and moves when it chooses to. The gazelle is prey. Always afraid of being hunted, moves in herds and ready to flee at any moment. But, both the lion and the gazelle, no matter what their differences are and what they feel like doing, need to run for their lives. One because it doesn't want to die of an attack, and the other because it doesn't want to die of hunger.

For most of history, this was the case. Animals were designed to move, and movement was not a choice. It was a necessity to stay alive. For us human beings too, this was the case until not too long ago. Even after we became a civilisation and we had figured out agriculture, we had to move to live and thrive. Work, of any and all forms, involved movement and usage of physical abilities. There was hardly anyone, except possibly a few of the royals, who could choose not to move and still get everything they needed, from food to safety to entertainment to comfort.

From then to now, we've come a long way. We have done well as a species. We have created a world where most of us can choose to move minimally and still live comfortably. Today, movement is a choice for many of us. It is indeed concerning that this sedentary lifestyle is causing health issues for billions. But, to be honest, the comfortable and convenient life we have created for ourselves is better than what humans of the past had to endure.

What is not great is that our bodies haven't adapted to this life of comfort, convenience and sedentarism. They need movement. Not just to stay alive and healthy, but also to stay sharp and happy. So, while movement seems like a choice, it really is not. Not if we want to live a life that is truly comfortable, pain-free and long.

The human body is one holistic unit. Every function is mutually dependent on at least one other function. There is no organ, cell or system in the body that functions as an independent contributor. So, naturally, in order to look, feel and function well, the body needs us to ensure that all our systems are working well. And movement is a big part of making this possible.

Physiologically, movement does four things that are important to our discussion:

- Enables energy oxidation (calorie burning) and utilisation, keeping the energy flow going
- Keeps bones, joints and muscles stimulated, thereby preventing immobility and atrophy
- Optimises blood circulation, which is the primary method of transporting oxygen, nutrients and hormones throughout the body
- Regulates hormones that affect metabolism, blood sugar regulation, digestion, muscle building, respiration and more

Psychologically, it does more. By helping regulate dozens of hormones including adrenalin, dopamine, leptin, ghrelin, adenosine and melatonin, it plays a role in regulating mood, appetite, satiety, alertness and even sleep.

As animals that are designed to move, we absolutely *need* movement. Maybe not to buy groceries, watch a movie or meet a friend anymore. But definitely to look, feel and function optimally, because movement is one of the cornerstones of physical, mental and emotional well-being.

> Be honest—what is your most dominant position during the day? Is it sitting? Barring exercise, how often do you move on a daily basis? Do you find yourself being active during the day?

#33   The three types of movement

At the highest level, we can classify movement as involuntary and voluntary. And under voluntary movements, we can classify movements into three types that are relevant to fitness—exercise, activities of daily life (ADL) and non-purposeful movement. Many terms and phrases are used to describe such movements and, sometimes, the categorisation could change too. But what matters is that we understand how they play a role in our lives.

Exercise is a common term, and we all know what it means. But, in its truest sense, it is actually a smartly packaged way of movement for the human body. Back in the day when we were still living in the wild, everyday movement included walking, running, jumping, pushing, pulling, climbing, hanging and crawling. Today, we don't have a need to do most of this. But our bodies still require us to do some of it. And exercise is our answer—a smart way of packaging all of these in a time-efficient and safe manner.

Activities of daily life (ADL) comprise essentially everything we do in a day outside of exercise, sports and any other activity aimed at physical fitness. Walking, climbing stairs, bathing, cleaning the house, procuring groceries, typing, writing, shopping and going to the movies are all examples. But do note that what qualifies as ADL varies from person to person and also from time to time. Each person's ADL is different based on who they are, where they live, what they do for work and more. Also, ADL requirements are different based on the time we live in. For example, a vegetable seller and a computer engineer have very different movement demands for work today. But, also, a vegetable seller in the 1970s would have walked a lot more for work than a vegetable seller in 2024.

Non-purposeful movement includes all the little movements we do without much thought. Fidgeting, facial expressions, scratching your head, tapping your feet and blinking are some examples. We do these without true awareness or a specific purpose. But they too need energy and they too are a part of our lives.

Out of these three types of movements, the first two are the ones that significantly affect health, strength, weight management and overall fitness. Instead of looking at them as things you just have to do because everyone from your mother to your doctor are asking you to, view them as simple tools. Tools to help you build that better version of yourself. If you can do that, you can make them a seamless part of your life and use them to positively improve your fitness and quality of life.

> If you could pick between exercising and doing hard manual labour every day, which one would you pick? Why?

#34 Anyone can exercise, and everyone should exercise

If you look back in time, you'll notice something very interesting about the relationship between activities of daily life (ADL) and exercise.

A very long time ago, the concept of exercise did not exist. All we needed was ADL. But ADL back then was not like the ADL of today. A normal day involved plenty of physical labour, stress and discomfort. Every day's ADL was as hard as (if not harder than) today's exercise. And so, exercise was not needed but everyone did the movements that are considered as exercise today.

This is why anyone *can* exercise. Exercise, when you remove all the bells and whistles, is just basic human movement done at different intensities. Squatting is the same as sitting and standing. Sprinting is, in essence, a faster way of covering distance by foot. Doing pull-ups is just hanging and pulling. And crawling is, well, just crawling. The reason it feels complicated and unsafe, and we actually need someone to teach us how to do these things, is because we are so out of touch with the basic human movements that we simply don't know how to do them anymore. And the reason the majority of the population today struggles to do a push-up or run for a few minutes is not because these are extremely hard things to do. It is because we have removed the need for such physical activity to a point where we are incapable of doing them.

In any case, back to history now.

Then there came a time (sometime post civilisation) when life was a little more comfortable for a few people. This resulted in the quantity and intensity of ADL reducing drastically and the need to increase intentional movement (aka exercise). Or a few people who didn't have to struggle for daily existence realised practice and training (also exercise) could improve something specific, and they started including different forms of intentional movement in their days. If not to help with health, it was most probably to help with work, warfare or hunting.

Fast forward to today, when for many people ADL and basic movement have become infrequent and low in intensity. And so, we have to really ramp up intentional movement to stay healthy and fit. We have no other choice.

As you can see, while our body's need for movement hasn't changed, how much we actually move has changed rather drastically, both in quality and quantity. Now, this is certainly all right. It is part of human evolution. It is expected, unavoidable and, in some ways, beneficial. But what is necessary is for us to understand this gap and fill it smartly. And the way to fill that gap is through conscious, voluntary movement.

This is why everyone *should* exercise. Not because everyone has to lose weight or look like a celebrity or perform like an athlete. But because everyone deserves a good quality life. And that just isn't possible without enough movement.

> How much has the quality, quantity, intensity and frequency of movement changed in your life over the last few years? Were you more active when you were younger?

#35 The four Ss of exercise

Exercise science is the scientific study of human movement that is performed to maintain or improve physical fitness. A large and wonderful discipline, a part of which is about what exercises need to be done, by whom, for what, when, at what intensities and for how long. But unless you are a specialist (competitive sportsperson, model, actor, etc.), you don't need to worry about the minutiae.

What you need from exercise is quite simple. You need the four Ss:

- Strength
- Stamina
- Speed
- Suppleness

Strength is your ability to apply force. You need strength to do anything in life. Holding a bottle of water or pushing a water tanker all by yourself. It is only a question of how much strength. Outwardly, you use your muscles and bones to do the final movement of strength application. But the process starts in your brain, right from the time you think about doing something, and involves every system in your body.

Stamina is your ability to sustain physical or mental effort. Effort that involves some form of discomfort for extended periods of time. So building stamina requires you to work on your ability to endure discomfort, that is, endurance.

Speed is your ability to do things at different rates. Doing something fast is about speed, but so is moving very slowly. And since doing things requires applying force, speed is about applying force at different rates, which is where 'power' comes in.

And *suppleness* is your ability to move in different planes and speeds, fluidly and without pain. This is a combination of being flexible in your muscles and mobile in your joints.

Though exercise has many forms and even more names, the end goal of all forms of exercise is the same—to optimally stimulate your muscles, joints, organs and organ systems. Bodybuilding, Zumba, sports, yoga, distance running, gymnastics, figure skating and more types of exercise exist. They are all different from one another in many, many ways. But one is not universally better than the other. Not in an absolute sense. They were all created with the intention to help improve fitness. And they all have their pros and cons.

It is simply about understanding what exactly *you* need and picking the ones that serve *you* best. If you are able to do that and address these four aspects of movement consistently, you can rest assured that you will see your fitness levels rise with time.

> Is there enough of each of the four Ss in your current training plan? Do you feel like you have a bias towards one or a few?

#36 Strength makes you better

Every one of the four Ss are important, and there is no denying it. Each person will find a higher need for some and lower need for some others, and we can debate for hours about which one of these is most important and never get to an agreement. But, with most people in mind, if we had to pick one to start with as the foundation on which we can build everything else, strength would be it.

Because strength essentially means using the muscles we have in our body to do work. Any work. And for those muscles to do work, connective tissue and bones also need to work. For this, enough oxygen, nutrients and hormones need to reach them, for which blood has to circulate optimally throughout the body. A lot of things need to come together for you to build foundational strength.

In a less physiological and more practical sense, strength makes you better at whatever it is that you do. And I'm not talking about just sport or fitness. More strength will help you do literally anything better. Whatever your profession—doctor, teacher, designer, accountant, engineer, student, writer—more strength can help you do it better. Whatever roles you play in life—parent, sibling, leader, friend, daughter, husband, partner—strength can help you play the role better. How? By enabling you to do what you need to do in your profession or role without getting fatigued quickly or hurting yourself unintentionally. Strength can make you a better version of yourself.

Imagine for a second that you wake up tomorrow morning with a severe weakness. Let's say your strength levels drop by 50 per cent across the board. How would you feel? Tired, weak, slow and hesitant. How would it feel to do everything you do in your day today with half the strength? Tiring, hard and laborious. And how good do you think you'll be in your profession and how well will you play the many roles that you play in your life? Not well, to say the least. This should help you understand and appreciate your current strength and how much it is silently serving you in your life today.

Now imagine if you end up increasing your strength levels by 50 per cent. Not overnight, but over the next few months. How would you feel? How would it feel to do everything you do in your day but with 50 per cent more strength? And how good do you think you'll be in your profession and how well will you play the many roles that you play in your life? No need to answer. I know you get it.

This is precisely why strength is critical for life and why we need to make strength training a regular part of our lives irrespective of who we are and what our short-term goals are.

> What do you do for a living? What are the different roles you play in your life? Can you envision how getting stronger can help you in your life every day?

#37 Strength training simplified

Strength training is like an ocean. It has dozens of different types of equipment. Thousands of different schools of thought. Millions of coaches and billions of enthusiasts with varying goals. But even with so many ways to strength train, the purpose of strength training is the same—to stimulate and strengthen the body as a whole. And as long as that happens, irrespective of what equipment, programme or exercise was used, it is considered strength training.

Resistance training is another name for strength training. If there is some form of resistance against which we're training, it can be considered resistance training. This resistance can come from anything, be it a barbell, a kettlebell, a dumbbell, resistance bands, a bag of potatoes or a piece of rock. Because the goal of using resistance is simply to stimulate and strengthen. The equipment matters less, the effort matters more.

But which muscles and which bones should we stimulate and strengthen? To be honest, all of them. A good strength training plan will include exercises that target all the major muscle groups in the body. And, as a result of this, all the bones and connective tissue that are connected to those muscles. But there are about 600 muscles and more than 200 bones in the human body! Finding an exercise for each of these and doing them regularly week after week sounds impossible. Luckily for us, it's not that complicated. In fact, it is so simple that literally four movement patterns can train most of these 600 muscles and 200+ bones.

While a bodybuilder might break the body down into multiple muscles and muscle groups and train them diligently, a normal person trying to build strength and health doesn't have to. For the bodybuilder, the primary goal is muscle development and symmetry. And for that it is important to stimulate and force growth in as many muscles as possible. But for most of us, the primary goal is to build overall strength and stay pain-free. This can be achieved by smartly working on a few compound movements that train a group of muscles as opposed to working on one muscle at a time.

For example, instead of training quadriceps, glutes, adductors, lower back musculature and transverse abdominus separately, you can focus on getting stronger on the squat. Because the squat is one move that can stimulate and strengthen all these muscle groups at the same time. Of course, we won't end up with thighs that are exploding with muscles, but that's not the goal in the first place. Similarly, instead of worrying about training the pectorals, triceps and deltoids, we can focus on getting stronger on the push-up, which will strengthen all three muscle groups. Such smart simplification can be done in such a manner that we cover the entire body. Just follow the 90–10 rule—work on the 10 per cent that give you 90 per cent of the results.

The simplest way to approach strength training is to pick the few movement patterns that train most of the functional muscles in the body and practise them regularly for a long time. The movement patterns that will cover the most muscle groups and give you the most bang for your buck are the squat, the hinge, the push and the pull. Add to this some core work, and you have a simple but solid strength training plan.

From each of these five categories, pick two to four moves. Make sure all of these are moves you know to do well and safely. This is your toolkit. The more tools you get, the more advanced your training can and will be. But it needn't be. You can start with whatever exercises you know how to do. With time and consistency, you can and will add more tools to this toolkit.

Squat—Any and all movements that require you to bend at your hips and knees will belong here. Examples are traditional squats, split squats, lunges, sumo squats and all jumps. Because any movement that flexes (bends) and extends the knee and hip joints will strengthen all the muscles around the knee and hip joints.

Hinge—Any and all movements that require you to bend a lot at the hip but minimally at the knee. Examples are deadlifts, good mornings, swings, cleans and snatches. These movements load the posterior chain—muscles on the back side of the body from the hamstring muscles, which are behind the thighs, till the trapezius muscles, which are on your upper back.

Push—Any and all movements that require you to push something away from you or push your body away from something. Examples are push-ups, bench press, overhead press, floor press, wall push, car push and med ball throws. All pushing movements strengthen the muscles of the chest, shoulders and back of the upper arm.

Pull—Any and all movements that require you to pull something towards you or pull your body towards something. Examples are rows, curls, pull-ups, face pulls, pull-downs and hangs. All pulling movements strengthen the muscles of the upper back, mid back, forearms and front of the upper arm.

Core—Any and all movements that strengthen your trunk. Examples are planks, hollow holds, crawls, weighted walks, carrys and bridges. Do keep in mind that loaded versions of the squat, hinge, push and pull also train the core. But given how critical core strength is for performance and everyday life, a little extra focus won't hurt.

Now, if you put the squat, hinge, push, pull and core together, you'll notice that you'll be stimulating and strengthening muscles on the front of your legs, back of your legs, lower back, mid back, upper back, chest, shoulders, forearms, upper arms and trunk. Honestly, that's everything you need to strengthen to live a strong and active life.

Once you have identified your toolkit, you can combine them in multiple ways and come up with innumerable plans of your own. While purists might disagree, the truth is that as long as you ensure that you balance your effort across all five categories and move with good technique, you simply cannot go wrong.

> If you had to create a very simple three days a week strength training plan for yourself using what you've read in this chapter, how would you do it? What moves would you pick?

#38 The three commandments of strength training

During my initial days of fitness, especially when I evolved from just running to a more holistic training plan that included lifting weights, I did what everyone does—pseudo bodybuilding. Basically, try and target different muscle groups on different days. Chest and back on Mondays, legs on Wednesdays and so on. It's not a bad approach by any means. But I realised quickly that what I really wanted was better functionality (strength, ease of movement, stamina, etc.) and not just bigger muscles. This is when I was exposed to a whole new world of lifting weights and many coaches who taught me most of the things I know today about strength training.

Of these coaches, two had a very deep impact on how I understood and embraced strength training—Dan John and Mark Rippetoe. They are both professional weightlifting coaches with decades of experience and have written multiple books analysing both the basics and the minutiae of lifting and strength training. I had the good sense to read everything they wrote, books and blogs alike, and had the privilege of being coached and certified by them on separate occasions.

Of all the things I learnt from them, the following three stuck with me. These three commandments have helped me immensely with my own training and with that of the thousands of people I have helped build immense everyday strength:

1. *Keep the goal the goal.* Don't be distracted by what other people are doing or think you should be doing. Be clear about *your* goals and *your* reasons for training. Remember them, and do only what you need to do to get to your goals, paying zero attention to what the next big thing is or what everyone else thinks is cool.
2. *The basics are everything.* Focus on them, get better at them and keep doing them for life. Whether you are looking to increase your strength by a little or transform into the strongest version of yourself, you don't need much more than the basics. It might sound too simple to be true. But it is true.
3. *Repetition matters.* The good reps, the bad reps and everything in between. So, no matter your reasons and excuses, do the work, do it consistently and do it properly.

> What is your goal with fitness? Have you been able to stay true to your goals or do you get distracted? Do you think you can find it in you to prioritise the basics over everything else?

#39 Do it well or don't do it at all

Any skill can be self-taught, and so can strength training. But only if you have the intent to learn and the time to practise. If you don't have either one, you're better off learning from an expert who is willing to teach. One way or the other, you must learn to move. Because quality will always trump quantity when it comes to movement.

Training with proper technique means using the right muscles to do the right job. And using the right muscles is always a safer and more effective approach. Let's take the squat, for example. The point of doing the squat is to strengthen the target muscle group, which are the quadriceps, glutes and adductors, while also strengthening some of the supporting muscles. But, if you work with a weight so heavy that your technique breaks and you end up using your lower back more than you should, then you're left with target muscle groups that were not loaded enough and a painful lower back, both of which are not productive. So, no matter what your goals are, what move you're doing and what load you're working with, always ensure that you're moving with good technique.

This is a mindset more than a precaution. The idea is simple—if you're doing something, do it well or don't do it at all. Apply this in every move and every rep. This will help you stay safe and continue to get progressively stronger in the long term.

If you think you can do this, that's wonderful. Pick your moves, put them together in a manner that makes sense to you and start training. Once you start, you'll figure out the right loading, understand how to optimise intensity and learn at every step along the way.

But if you're not sure you can do this by yourself, please work with a coach who can teach you how to move with proper technique. This is no different from learning any skill from a teacher. If the teacher is a good one, your path will certainly be safer, faster and more effective. Today, there are plenty of wonderful coaches out there who will care about your goals, be kind to you, get you started from wherever you are currently and genuinely support you in your fitness journey, even if you are a complete beginner. You just need to care enough to find a coach who brings the best out of you.

> How good is your technique when you train? Do you let it deteriorate as you get tired or do you make it a point to move only with good technique? Do you feel you can learn proper form for all exercises and execute it consistently? Or would you do better with a coach?

#40 Stamina is what keeps you going

Every day we need to put in effort to live. Both physically and mentally, we need to do things and often without a break. We have many roles to play and endless chores to do. From the moment we wake, we are active. Some of it we call work and most of it we don't. But all of it requires some amount of mental and physical effort. And in order to be able to do this day after day and do it better with every progressing day, we need stamina—the ability to sustain prolonged physical or mental effort.

While movement is visibly physical, it affects the body both physically and mentally and can influence our physical and mental abilities positively or negatively. So, training ourselves to be enduring and resilient is important not just for fitness but also for life. Hardship is a part of life, and the more ready we are to endure it, the better we can navigate through life. And one way to learn to endure hardship is through endurance training. This will result in building stamina, which will help you be more tough and resilient, not just physically but mentally too. And all of this will certainly help you take better control of your life through the ups and, more importantly, the downs.

Physiologically, stamina building from consistent endurance training can be a significant contributor towards

- better heart health
- energy balance control

- improved metabolism
- improved sport performance
- reduced daily fatigue from activities of daily life (ADL).

Practically though, if you really consider life today, stamina is the part of fitness that you'll need most commonly. Playing with your kids and pets, climbing up a few flights of stairs, carrying your own bags at an airport, running to catch a train or flight, or sprinting to help someone in need are all situations we may find ourselves in more often than we will find ourselves trying to lift a 200-kilo object or climb a wall or crawl under a barbed wire.

Emotionally, learning to tolerate discomfort for long periods of time results in a sense of accountability and achievement. It teaches us how to keep going even when the going gets tough. It builds character. And most importantly, the process of building stamina gives us an opportunity to learn about approaching hardships in life using fitness as a sandbox for life.

> What do you need physical stamina for in your life today? What about mental stamina? And do you feel working on your physical stamina could help you mentally and emotionally too?

#41 The different types of endurance

Broadly speaking, there are three types of endurance you should be familiar with—cardiovascular or aerobic endurance, anaerobic endurance and muscular endurance.

Aerobic endurance is the ability to sustain work for long periods of time at a low intensity. It is usually called 'cardio' or cardiovascular endurance, because this type of endurance training strengthens the heart (which is a muscle). It is also called 'aerobic endurance' because this type of endurance is done at an intensity (and heart rate) low enough for the body to be able to take in and use oxygen continuously. Typically, this involves activities like walking, hiking, jogging, running, swimming and cycling, but anything that involves using energy at a low intensity will qualify as aerobic endurance training. So, technically, if you can move your hands and legs around for an hour while keeping your heart rate in the right range, you are working on your aerobic endurance.

What is this heart rate range? Usually, to train aerobic endurance, you want your heart rate to be between 60 to 80 per cent of your maximum heart rate (MHR). And your MHR is simply 220−age. There are more accurate and complicated ways to calculate this, but let's not get lost in the details. For all practical purposes, training to a heart rate that is higher than 60 per cent of MHR and keeping it under 80 per cent MHR is ideal for aerobic endurance. If you aren't familiar or comfortable with heart rate monitors and smart watches, simply train at an intensity that allows you to speak full sentences mid-activity, with mild discomfort but without gasping for breath. This will ensure you stay in the aerobic training zone.

Anaerobic endurance is the ability to sustain work in the absence of oxygen. As you know, our bodies need a steady supply of oxygen to function. At any point of time during the day, we need to take in oxygen at a rate that is sufficient to keep all the necessary functions running. This is why our rate of breathing and heart rate change throughout the day based on what we do. When we sleep, we are doing the least possible work, and so our breathing and heart rates are at their lowest. When we sit and work, these rates are still low, but higher than when we sleep. When we walk, do chores and so forth, these rates increase and keep rising as the intensity of the work we do increases.

Consider the difference between walking and sprinting. We do both for the same reason—to cover distance. When we walk, we take our time and put in minimal effort. Our heart and breathing rates increase slightly. When we sprint, we rush and put in as much effort as possible in a short time. As a result, our heart and breathing rates shoot up to a point where our hearts are beating at two to three times the normal rate and we are gasping for breath. We do this because the body is asking for more oxygen in order to sustain the functions necessary to keep sprinting because everything in our bodies, especially our muscles, needs oxygen to function.

Unlike aerobic endurance, anaerobic endurance training involves working at a high intensity for shorter durations. And the higher the intensity, the shorter the duration. So, sprints, interval training, HIIT (high intensity interval training), plyometrics, mile repeats, hill runs, timed metabolic conditioning workouts and shuttle runs are all examples of anaerobic endurance training.

Muscular endurance is not about heart or breathing rate but the ability of a particular muscle to work without getting fatigued. For example, being able to do one bicep curl with a very heavy weight is a display of strength. But being able to do 100 bicep curls with a light weight is a display of muscular endurance. While there is no definitive rep range to define this (because muscular strength improves muscular endurance and vice versa), training your muscles to endure discomfort for as long as possible is what muscular endurance is about.

If all this seems too technical for you, don't worry. If you're a professional athlete, you'll certainly need to understand more about endurance and dedicate a large part of your training towards it with specific protocols and goals. But if you're someone looking to improve the way you look, feel and function, what matters most is consistency. So, keep it simple, do the work regularly, and your endurance has no choice but to improve.

> Do you consider yourself a professional athlete or a weekend warrior? What type of endurance matters most to you?

#42 Embrace discomfort, build stamina

If there is one aspect of fitness where you can 'feel' the results almost immediately, it is stamina. Unlike strength, stamina can be quite volatile. A simple cold or a couple of weeks of inactivity can cause a perceivable and often significant drop. But all you need is just a few weeks of consistent training to see a spike in your stamina.

This is not necessarily good or bad news. Because while temporary ups and downs are expected, in the long term, to truly improve stamina, you need to do consistent endurance training. To do that, you need to do three things.

First, *pick the discomfort*. There are way too many options to improve stamina through endurance training. Everything from jogging to Zumba to power yoga—literally anything that increases and decreases your heart rate in a structured manner—will do the job. So, as the first step, find the activity that you enjoy doing. In any and all of them, your heart and breathing rate will rise and fall and you will surely feel discomfort. But if you pick an activity that you enjoy, like dancing or playing a sport or hiking with friends or anything that has an element of joy, you will pay less attention to the discomfort and focus more on having fun. This will help in getting work done and, more importantly, in sustaining it in your life for much longer.

Second, *schedule the discomfort*. Because, let's face it, if you don't schedule it, you're not going to do it. It can be a run by yourself or a game of pickleball with your friends or a dance class. If you don't actually plan to do it, you're not going to do it. And it's not your fault. We are simply not wired to seek discomfort. In fact, it's quite the opposite. We are wired to avoid it. So, unless we make a conscious effort to exercise, with the understanding that putting ourselves through discomfort now will result in comfort later, we won't do it. Delayed gratification doesn't come naturally.

Third, *embrace the discomfort*. It's not going to be easy or fun at first. This is where some basic discipline comes into play. If you can stay disciplined enough to do the work for the first few days, something wonderful will happen. A habit will form. And suddenly, it won't feel as hard anymore. And once you start doing the work regularly and understand the process of improvement, you will be able to consider both the discomfort and the pleasure. You will be able to reason with yourself as to why you need to go through discomfort in order to seek pleasure. With time, resistance will reduce and you will focus less on the instant discomfort and more on the delayed gratification. And you will be rewarded with feelings of euphoria soon after, higher energy levels later in the day and improved fitness for life.

> How do you like endurance training? Be it a sport or dance or running or HIIT, do you enjoy doing it? Or do you just do it because you have to? Or do you not do it at all? What change would you like to make to your routine in relation to endurance training?

#43 Speed and power

There are things we need to do slowly and delicately, and things we need to do quickly and with much force. But more important is the ability to change speeds and apply different levels of force at will. This ability to control the rate at which we move and apply force is natural and one that evolution intended for us to have in order to survive and thrive. Speed and power are indeed a part of the fabric of life, and more than we realise.

Imagine a scenario where you need speed or power. Say you're in a rush and need to run up a few flights of stairs to fetch something. Or say you have to force a jammed door open. It is obvious why you need to act fast and apply power. But there are also scenarios when you need to be slower and softer than normal, say when you're drawing or setting the table.

While the former is considered 'fast' and the latter is considered 'slow', they are both just actions done at different speeds and levels of force. The ability to control our movements and calibrate them to the task at hand needs to be consciously developed for fitness, health and life. Specifically from a fitness perspective, training for speed and power has a whole host of benefits. Other than the functional improvements in life from directly increasing your control, working on your speed and power will help with the following.

Strength—Strength is about applying force, and power is about applying force quickly. Working on your power-generation capabilities will indirectly but significantly help improve your strength levels.

Energy flow—We burn calories when we exert ourselves. Of all the different types of movement, fast and powerful movements demand the most from our bodies and brains and so burn the most calories per unit of time.

Agility—In addition to how fast we move and how powerful we can be, how quickly we can think and react is also a skill that we use in life. While agility training is a world of its own, training for speed and power will teach the brain to think fast, send signals more efficiently and improve reaction time.

Training for speed and power may not be as common as strength or stamina. But it can be extremely beneficial. While not mandatory, it is something that will truly elevate your training without complicating it.

> Have you realised that different levels of speed and power are a regular part of your day? When you run up the stairs, cut your child's nails, lift weights at the gym, flip a bubble top can, carefully move the table etc. What other scenarios can you think of that require you to speed up or down or use more or less power?

#44 Training for speed and power

The moment we hear 'speed' and 'power', we think of words like 'race', 'competition' or 'fight'. I'd like to change that association to three less combative words—'fun', 'simple' and 'strong'. Because improving your speed and power is actually quite simple, can be very fun and will make you feel strong in everyday life.

Speed training is about doing things fast without compromising movement quality. Let's say running is your chosen activity and you want to increase your running speed. How do you train for it? The most obvious way to do it is by running fast. And it's true. The simplest way to increase speed is to do speed work in your choice of activity or sport. To see improvements in speed and power in a sport, martial arts or just everyday activity, working on technique, improving strength and stamina and optimising mobility are all necessary. But the primary requirement is to do direct speed work. This is a simple step to start for most and maybe the only step needed for many.

But when you do speed work, it is important to keep the following in mind.

- *Ramp up.* Speed and power training are both explosive in nature. But you cannot go from being barely warmed up to explosive. At least, not safely. It's important to warm up and then ramp up in intensity gradually before doing explosive work.

- *Stick to what you know.* You can safely generate speed and produce power only using movement patterns you are very familiar and comfortable with. A professional tennis player might have a 200 kmph serve, but if they tried bowling in cricket, the ball would travel much slower. Similarly with exercise, you need to know how to squat (or swing or press or cycle or swim) well before you can use it as a power- or speed-building tool.
- *Keep it short and powerful.* Intensity and duration are inversely proportional. If one is high, the other has to be low. Speed and power work are high in intensity. So, it is important to keep the duration short. Based on your fitness levels and choice of activity, this can be anywhere from just a few seconds per set (Olympic lifting, 40-yard sprint, broad jumps, for example) to a couple of minutes of hard work (400 m or longer sprints, 100 m or longer swims, stair climbs, for example). But, as a general rule, you need to try to maintain power and speed at the level it needs to be during all reps or the entire duration of your activity. In other words, when the power drops, you stop.
- *Be consistent.* Like everything else, speed and power are abilities that your body builds with time and practice. It involves plenty of systems, hormones and movements coming together in a coordinated fashion. During the first few times, you may not feel fast or powerful. In fact, you may find yourself uncoordinated when trying to move at high speed. But, don't feel ashamed and don't give up. With consistency you'll be able to see obvious improvements, which will have an observable effect in the way you look, feel and function.

Speed and power training can be done as a standalone session or can be trained along with strength, either before or after your work sets. Make it a regular part of your training, and it will cause a significant spike in your ability to move better.

> Do you currently have a power or speed component in your training? If so, how do you enjoy it? Does it help you with other aspects of your training (such as strength and stamina)? If not, how do you feel about including it?

#45 To be strong, you need to be supple

Quality of movement is less about strength and power and more about flexibility and mobility.

'Supple' doesn't have the same impressive ring to it as 'strong' or 'powerful' does. But, in reality, one can't become too strong or powerful without basic suppleness. And to be functionally strong, fast and powerful, a high degree of suppleness is an absolute requirement.

A professional tennis player's ankles when she slides on the court. The strength and grace of a gymnast when he glides over those parallel bars. The alignment of a swimmer's joint stacking before, during and after each stroke. All these are examples of how strength, speed, stamina and suppleness come together, resulting in incredible physical feats. And this isn't limited to high movement activities either. Powerlifters require a lot of mobility to do what they do safely too.

You may not want to do any of this, and that's fine. But if fitness is something you're after because you want to improve your quality of life, that's not going to happen without some degree of suppleness. Because flexibility and mobility are what allow you to build strength, power and endurance and help you move safely without injury or pain. This is why 'supple enough' is something everyone should aspire to be.

You may have heard of 'range of motion'. Active range of motion (ROM) basically refers to how much your body is capable of moving without resistance or pain. Every joint has a certain active ROM and passive ROM. This is not a number but a range. As long as you're in the range that is right for you based on your age, you're safe and good to go. But the problem is most people are not.

Let's do a couple of quick tests. Can you squat all the way down and hold that position for a minute without any discomfort or pain? Can you touch your toes without bending your knees? Can you reach behind your head and touch the opposite shoulder blade?

These are a few of the hundreds of tests available to check for functional mobility. But the best and most relevant tests are pain and movement quality. In other words, if you are supple enough to move as well as necessary (gracefully, seamlessly, quickly and controllably) in your life and activity of choice and don't have any limitations or pain, you're good. If not, we need to loosen you up a little.

> Are you able to move well and without any pain? How mobile are you in your joints? How flexible are you in your muscles? Do you see how the previous three questions are related?

#46 Supple enough

You may not want to become as supple as a leopard, but you don't want to walk around like Frankenstein either. Mobility and flexibility, while not the most exciting aspects of fitness, are certainly important ones, and you definitely want to be supple enough to not hurt yourself.

Here is how you can improve your suppleness without overanalysing it.

Move often. Before we even get to the specifics of flexibility and mobility, we need to address something very basic—sedentarism. A lack of movement will make you feel tight and creaky. Remember, our bodies are designed to move. Without the necessary movement, there is not enough lubrication in the joints. And when there isn't enough synovial fluid (joint lubricant) circulation, there is stiffening and shrinking of cartilage—a flexible connective tissue that cushions joints. Moreover, the lack of optimal blood circulation makes it harder for muscles to get the nutrients they need. So, for more reasons than one, move and move often.

Move with good technique. Another important requirement for basic mobility (but not necessarily flexibility) is moving with proper technique whenever you exercise. All our joints have a certain optimal range, and this becomes even more important when we load movements. So, when strength training or doing fast work, move in the optimal ranges of motion (ROM). Because moving in ranges outside the optimal ROM stresses joints and loads muscles improperly, causing muscular imbalances and joint pain. And moving in the optimal ROM consistently will improve active range with time.

Mobilise before training. Remember that exercise is regular movement but done at a higher intensity. You use the same joints and muscles to sit on a couch and stand back up as you do for a box squat with 100 kilos on your back. But joints also need to be prepped before being loaded up. So, start every training session by mobilising the joints that are going to be used. Simply use common sense here. Are you going to run? Mobilise your ankles, knees, hips and spine. Push-ups? Wrist, elbows and shoulder. You get the idea.

Stretch after training. When you exercise, your muscle fibres contract and relax. It is this contraction and relaxation that enables you to work. The more intense your training, the more intense the contraction and relaxation. As a result, your muscles become tense. And stretching helps to reduce this muscle tension. Here too, it helps to not complicate things. Think about which muscles you used during your session, and stretch them for about 30 to 60 seconds each. As a general rule, the bigger muscles like your lats, quadriceps, glutes and hamstrings need more stretching time while the smaller ones like your biceps, triceps, calf and forearm muscles are happy with less.

> How would you like to incorporate mobility and flexibility training in your life? Would you prefer doing something specific like yoga, or would you rather add mobility before training, optimal ROM during training and stretching after training?

#47 Structure your training, one week at a time

Fitness as a problem is solved. We know enough about training and nutrition. There are more than enough training programmes that provide solid results. There are enough coaches who know enough to guide you to get those results. And there are enough gyms, training spaces and equipment using which you can safely train for those results. Simply said, if you show up regularly and do the work, you will see results. There are no two ways about it.

The only problem is most people don't show up to do the work. So, while fitness is technically solved, consistency is not. And until we solve consistency, results will be elusive even in the presence of everything else.

The first step in solving consistency is creating a sustainable weekly training schedule. This should be one that you can stick to without much stress and without having to make too many compromises. If you can figure out one such schedule for yourself, given your life, your commitments and your constraints, you will have set yourself up for success.

Here are a few ways to structure your week of training such that you address all of the four Ss in a balanced manner.

- If you can train only one day every week, do a combination of strength and stamina. Start with 5–10 minutes of mobility. Then spend 20–30 minutes on strength. Move on to 10–20 minutes of stamina-building work. And finish with 5–10 minutes of flexibility work. What exactly you want to do in each of these sections is up to you. And I hope the previous chapters have given you enough clarity to start.

- If you can train only two days every week, either do two days of the above or do one day of strength work with 15–20 minutes of speed and power work to finish, and one day of pure stamina-building work. Make sure you spend 10 minutes on mobility before and 10 minutes on flexibility after training on both days.
- If you can train three days a week, you can do two days of strength and stamina combo plus one day of dedicated speed and power training. Or you can do two days of strength work with speed and power training included plus one day of stamina-building work. Mobility and flexibility will be a part of all training days, irrespective of how many days you train.
- If you can train four to five days a week, you can do two days of pure strength work, one to two days of stamina-building work and one to two days of speed and power work.
- And if you can train six days a week, you can do an even split of two days each of strength, stamina and speed. Or you can bring in a bias by training one aspect for three days, another aspect for two days and the last one for one day.

The only other thing you need to remember is to not train the same aspect on two consecutive days because your body needs time to recover. So, if Monday is strength, let Tuesday be something that is not strength, and so on.

There are just way too many permutations and combinations that you can come up with to create a training structure. And as always, the specifics matter less. What matters more is that you find a structure that works for you. So, keep it simple, start with what you can do today and focus only on consistency. Everything else will eventually fall in place.

> What would your ideal training week look like? How many days can you afford to dedicate towards training presently? How would you bring in the four Ss?

#48 The 10,000-step solution

Exercise is hard to do for most of us—physically and logistically. So hard that on a day when we have exercised it feels like we've done all the activity necessary for the day. In fact, I used to feel exactly this way. On days that I exercised, I would have this beautiful sense of achievement and completion and I wouldn't feel the need to move for anything else throughout the day. And it felt justified. But the unfortunate truth is that, irrespective of whether we exercise or not, activities of daily life (ADL) are important because exercise and ADL serve different purposes.

To recap, ADL is any and all movement outside of exercise. Today, given how much convenience most of us enjoy, the only movement we do outside of exercise is walking. And the amount of walking we *need* to do is laughably little. In fact, we don't have a reason to walk anymore! Everything is delivered to us. Groceries, food, clothing, perfumes, supplements, medicine, sports, movies, flowers and even fitness are now home delivered. All we need to do is click a few times on that little smartphone of ours that we all never ever part with. What a great time to be alive!

An average adult living in a city walks about 2,000 to 3,000 steps per day today. This is when no conscious effort is made and when movement happens only when there is a need. And this is the average. That means there are people who walk much less than that. If you are in this range or below, it's OK. This is just how our life is structured today and maybe there wasn't much you could have done about it. Until now.

The more we move, the better it is for us. And since walking is the only form of movement that is applicable to us today, the more we walk the better it is. The 10,000 steps number has been popularised lately, but that's nothing more than a nice looking, round number. The fact is that every step counts. Walking helps us correct posture, improve blood circulation and also burn some extra energy. To be specific, for every 1,000 steps you take, you burn about 25–50 kcal based on age, body weight and speed of walking. And if weight loss or maintenance is a goal for you, walking 7,000–15,000 steps per day can contribute to an extra 200–600 calories burnt per day, which is rather significant.

But all this boils down to one simple but inconvenient action item—walk more. The easiest way to make this possible involves two mindset changes.

First, you have all day to walk. Most people make the mistake of trying to get all their steps in one shot. Meaning, they try to go for a long walk. The problem with this is that we're approaching activity like exercise. And if we miss that window for whatever reason, we end up doing little to no activity on that day. Instead, think about accumulating your steps throughout the day. Think 'I have 16 hours to walk', because every waking hour is available for you to walk. Instead of cramming everything within a shorter time slot, you can space it out throughout the day and let the steps accumulate. A few minutes of walking at different points of time throughout the day will give you a better chance of walking more and sustaining this effort.

Second, be greedy for activity. To really increase your daily activity, it is not enough to just try to walk more. You need to start thinking and acting like an active person. An active person is someone who looks forward to movement and uses every opportunity available to move. Be that person. Take the trash out, walk to the store, always take the stairs, walk for no reason, take the dog out, walk when you're taking a phone call and catch up with a friend over a walk instead of over cake.

While walking doesn't qualify as exercise for most able people, it's an underrated activity. With a little bit of strategy, you can certainly use it to your advantage. But, remember, we don't have a real reason to walk anymore, but we still need the movement. So, make up reasons, find opportunities, do what you have to do and get it done.

> Do you know how much you walk on a daily basis? Do you make an effort to be more active during the day? How can you create more opportunities for yourself to walk more during the day?

SECTION 4

SLEEP

#49 Sleep is when the magic happens

If there was a drug available in the market that guaranteed a spike in energy levels, increased strength and endurance, better mental clarity and acuity, less anxiety and much better skin, most of us would most probably take it. And if it were completely safe and cost close to nothing, we most definitely would.

The good news is that it is available. And it is indeed safe and free. The not-so-good news is that we are not making the most of it. Sure, it isn't available in pill form. And we do need to do a little work to reap all these benefits. But the rewards are so disproportionate to the efforts that it is a no-brainer to use it well.

Sleep. The one thing that is capable of completely transforming how we look, feel and function. In fact, the only thing that has the power to influence the overall systemic functioning of our bodies, our emotions and our behaviours at a large scale.

Imagine yourself driving to work. The night before, you slept really well. You woke up this morning feeling physically energetic and mentally calm. You were nice to your family, didn't get triggered by anything on social media, got in some movement, made good food choices and happily hopped into your car to get to work. As you're driving, a cyclist cuts in suddenly. You swerve just at the right time, saving yourself and the cyclist from an accident. You stop, look at the guy, check if he's OK and wave calmly. But the guy is mad. He frowns and curses at you as he flees the scene. You don't mind it much. You think, 'Poor guy, he must be in a hurry or in a bad mood', smile and move on to the rest of your day.

Now, imagine the same scenario on a different day. The night before, you worked late, ate late, maybe had a drink or two and went to bed late. You woke up this morning with insufficient and poor-quality sleep, feeling low in energy and irritable. You didn't have a great time at home because you were grumpy and got into a little tiff with your spouse. You were tired and not motivated to train. So you decided to feel better by eating something fun and delicious. Something that makes you feel comfortable immediately but lethargic later. You get into your car worrying about how you're going to handle everything you have on your plate for the day—meetings, project deadlines, chores, kids, social events and what not. As you're driving, a cyclist cuts in suddenly. You somehow manage to swerve just at the right time, saving yourself and the cyclist from an accident. But the guy is mad. He frowns and curses at you. What do you think happens next?

The difference in how well our body and the various organs and systems function with and without sufficient sleep is pretty crazy. Because, as organic beings, we need a certain balance between stress and recovery for us to thrive. This is true of any animal, and especially with animals that rely on their physical, mental and emotional abilities to live, work and create together. Stress happens throughout the day. When we work, when we learn, when we love and even when we do nothing. Our bodies are always working, in one way or the other. It is when we sleep that it all comes together.

Sleep is when our memory improves.

Sleep is when our muscles repair, recover and get stronger.

Sleep is when our breathing slows down and cell repair speeds up.

Sleep is when our experiences from the day are moulded into learnings for life.

Sleep is when we play out scenarios to learn to deal with emotions.

Sleep is when our various organs and systems get their break.

Sleep is when we process all the information from the day.

Sleep is when the magic happens.

Sleep more. Sleep better. Please.

Think of a time when you were sleep deprived. How did you behave that day? Did you feel physically active or tired? Were you mentally sharp or sluggish? Were you able to be patient and kind with the people around you or did you find yourself getting frustrated and annoyed at little things?

How much did you sleep last night? How well did you sleep? How about the last week and month?

In general, how much importance do you give sleep? Do you prioritise it and ensure you get enough or do you sleep for whatever time you get?

#50 Tired but wired

Have you seen the number of funny memes and reels about people not being able to sleep even though they are tired and sleepy? Well, it's quite a lot and growing. And this is alarming, because what such funny memes do is normalise behaviours that only a few people think they are going through. By doing so, they help us realise that such occurrences are very common and that many others are going through it.

Outside of 'hard evidence' like memes and reels, scientific surveys and studies also tell us the same story. That most of us today want to sleep more but we're just unable to. Why does that happen? How can we fix it? And how do we actually get that beauty, strength, energy and vitality this wonder-drug promises?

There is a simple reason behind why most of us struggle to fall asleep or stay asleep. The good news is that this may not be psychological, hormonal or genetic. So, it isn't something to be worried about or medically treated. The not-so-good news though is that it is something that only you can address, and it requires you to make a few changes that you may not be willing to make very readily.

Lifestyle. Such a simple and harmless word. It essentially means the way in which we live our daily life. But, as a concept, it is so powerful that it defines what our days are filled with and determines how our health will pan out in the future. It is this lifestyle that determines how energetic we can feel, what metabolic disease we may have to deal with, how consistent or inconsistent we can be and how easily we can fall asleep and how refreshing this sleep can be.

Theoretically speaking, there are many lifestyle factors that can affect sleep. Work hours, sleep time, caffeine consumption, meal times, screen time, exercise intensity and exercise time are some examples. That said, it is very possible that most of these factors are already in place for you. But, if you feel your sleep can be better, the first thing you need to do is understand that there is at least one thing in your lifestyle that you can change or improve. The second thing you need to do is be prepared to make that change or improvement.

There are certainly some who have sleep issues that are physiological, psychological or hormonal and need medical intervention. But most of us today can certainly improve both the quality and quantity of our sleep by making simple lifestyle changes. So, unless you are one of the very few who need to visit a sleep clinic, be assured that you have the power and the opportunity to drastically improve your sleep and, as a result, improve everything from your mood to energy levels to health to rate of weight loss.

> How often do you find yourself feeling tired and sleepy but unable to shut off your mind? Why do you think that happens to you? And what part of your lifestyle do you think you need to change in order to address this?

#51 Comfortable, cold, dark and quiet

You need a larger refrigerator. One that is large enough to fit you, a mattress, some pillows, a sheet and a comforter to cover yourself. Every night, all you need to do is open the door to this refrigerator, walk in, get comfortable and sleep. Because your first and most basic step towards better sleep is making sure your sleep environment is optimal. And optimal here means comfortable, cold, dark and quiet.

Where do you find a refrigerator that is big enough to fit all of this? Well, your bedroom certainly has the potential to become one. And we're going to learn how to make it the best place to sleep.

Comfort is something we all need in order to rest. From the early human's invention of 'nests' made out of grass and leaves to today's most advanced mattress designs, we humans have come up with a variety of options so we can be as comfortable as possible when we retire for the night. The reasons are obvious, and there is no one right way to do this. *You* need to find ways to make *your* sleeping environment comfortable and free of disturbance.

Comfortable doesn't mean your bed has to be fluffy like a cloud or something invented by NASA. It needs to be comfortable enough to sleep well through the night and wake up without any aches or pains. And free of disturbance doesn't necessarily mean you crawl into a sleeping cubicle that is protected against all sound, light and humans. It simply means you need to prioritise your sleep enough to ensure you don't have any obvious disturbances in your sleeping area.

Cold is a relative term. But research tells us that the optimal sleeping temperature is between 18 and 25 degrees Celsius. Of course, this varies from person to person based on preference, age, body temperature, air circulation, material of sheets used and more. But it is very clear that we sleep better when it is cold than when it is warm. So, based on where you live and what your constraints are, play around with the variables that are under your control (AC temperature, thickness and material of sheets, fan speed, etc.) and find the setting that provides you with the most restful sleep.

Dark, too, is a relative term. But, for restful sleep, darker is better. And that means the more light-proof your sleeping environment is, the better your sleep quality. This is because our eyelids are actually quite translucent. They can pick up light activity (and relay information to the brain) even when our eyes are closed. So try and remove any and all light sources. Obviously, remove all direct light sources like bulbs, TVs, displays, etc. But also try to address light that seeps in from other places. For example, light from a streetlamp outside the house can't be turned off but can be kept out by using blackout curtains or blinds. When it is not possible to keep light out of the room, a sleep mask is a great substitute.

Quiet is not a relative term, but it has an interesting relation to sleep. Just like how light affects our ability to sleep, sound does too. Some of us are light sleepers, and we wake up even at the sound of the doorknob. But some of us can sleep through a riot. Some of us *need* pin-drop silence, while some others *need* white noise (like the fan running) to fall asleep. So, it helps to keep this relative and remove the sounds that affect us and add the sounds that help us. When removing disturbing sounds is not under your control, earplugs can come in handy.

While simple to understand, executing these changes may not be straightforward. Sometimes these changes can be easy, and all you need to do is move things around a bit. But sometimes these can be hard, especially if you have a partner who snores, a child who is unwell, a neighbour who is a night owl or if you live on a busy street. So, don't overthink it and let it bother you too much. Instead, make an effort to try and improve your sleeping environment by as much as you can and move on.

> Take a moment to think about your sleeping environment. Would you say it is comfortable? Do you find it to be warm or too cold or just right? Is it dark and quiet?

#52 The rhythm we all dance to

Envision a busy factory. In different areas of the factory, different machines that are part of different systems work tirelessly. Some receive, some clean, some produce, some destroy, some protect and some expel. Everything works seamlessly. For the factory to function like this sustainably, there need to be periods of maximal usage and periods of minimal or zero usage. It is during this downtime that maintenance and repair can happen. Without it, the periods of high productivity won't and can't happen.

The human body is like a factory. It works at different intensities at different times. And sleep is the downtime when maintenance and repair can be done. During this time, most functions are still running, but they at a low intensity. Heart rate is reduced, digestion is paused, respiration rate drops, and everything except the essential functions necessary for repair and recovery are downgraded. The brain too is something that needs this downtime. In fact, the brain is at the front and centre of all this. If the brain (and mind) is not calm and ready to rest, your body simply cannot sleep.

The most important part of sleep is calming the mind and helping the brain relax. For this, we need to reduce stimulation. This is important because the brain is designed to take in any and all stimuli as input, make sense of it and make us aware of it. For example, if you're trying to sleep and your puppy keeps pawing at you, you can't sleep. Because your little guy is stimulating you through touch and you 'feel' it. Same deal when there is a loud noise when you're trying to doze off or when someone pours cold water on your face when you're sleeping. A stimulus occurs, your brain processes it, you feel something and are stimulated and, hence, disturbed.

The most powerful way to stimulate the brain is light. As animals who evolved through millions of years, we are tuned to react to light as we were in the wild. We have a deep connection with the sun. Our bodies and brains are used to depending on it as a guide.

Our eyes, which are the primary light sensors, are actually an extension of the brain, and the only part of the brain that is actually exposed. And, more interestingly, our eyelids are just a thin layer of skin and are translucent. So, when the sun rises, its light acts as a stimulus. The optic nerve senses it, the brain processes it and understands it is morning light. It then sends signals to the rest of the body to ramp up the functioning of other organs and releases cortisol and other hormones, enabling us to move around and live. In the evening, once the sun sets, there is mostly darkness with some moonlight. This light is much lower in intensity and more orange in colour. This is sensed by the optic nerve and processed by the brain, and information that it is time to wind down is sent to the rest of the body. Cortisol production is pulled down and melatonin is secreted, enabling us to slow down, reduce activity and bodily functions, and gradually fall asleep.

This twenty-four-hour internal clock in our brain that regulates cycles of alertness and sleepiness by responding to light changes in our environment is what we call the circadian rhythm.

> How aligned are you with the circadian rhythm? Do you find that you feel better when you wake up around sunrise and wind down stressful activities when the sun goes down? Or do you prefer staying up late and waking up late?

#53 Harness the power of light

We live in a time that seems very futuristic and different from the time our bodies were designed. But we still rely on the same old mechanism, stimuli and signals. And that's why light is still such a powerful stimulator. It still has the power to control when, how much and how well we can sleep. So, learning to use it in our favour is a skill that will serve us well in many ways and for the rest of our lives.

But, how do you harness the power of light? Do these three things:

1. *Get sunlight every morning.* Within an hour of waking up, get about 10–20 minutes of sun exposure. You don't have to and should not look at the sun directly. But spend time in the sunlight in the morning. Don't overthink it and don't change too much in your day. Keep it simple and see how you can make this a part of your morning. You can do this on your balcony as you drink your morning beverage or go for a walk or exercise outdoors or even just stand around in the sun for a few minutes.
2. *Switch to orange lights and dim it down at night.* Once the sun is down, start making two changes inside the house—switch to orange light and make it dim. So, low-wattage orange bulbs instead of tube lights. By about 8 p.m., try to make sure all the lighting at home is orange and dim. How dim? As dim as possible, with just enough light to not bump into things is ideal. But take a call based on your home and family. As always, embrace the concept. Go easy on the specifics.

3. *Stay away from blue light before bed.* Screens emit blue light. And this applies to all screens—TVs, smartphones, tablets and computers. This light is very similar to the light from the sun. So when we're exposed to bright blue light (especially, when screens are bright and close to us), we confuse the brain. This messes with the balance between cortisol and melatonin, which manifests as difficulty in falling asleep. It doesn't stop there. Exposure to blue light before bed also affects the quality of our sleep during the night. This doesn't mean you need to do away with screens. It is almost impossible to do so in today's world, where we use these devices for everything from entertainment to education to shopping to banking. All it means is that you need to be smart about your screen use at night—switch to night mode or use a blue light filter (available on almost all smartphones), reduce the brightness, reduce how long you're staring into a screen and, most importantly, consume content that is calming and not stimulating.

In short, expose yourself to blue light in the morning and protect yourself from blue light at night. It's as simple as that.

> Reality check—do you get any sun exposure in the morning? And how long do you stare into your screen every night?
>
> Does switching to dim, orange lights at night seem possible in your household? Are you willing to try it for a few days to assess how it improves your sleep?

#54 It's warm, brown and bitter, but it makes your brain 'brain' better

The world's most commonly used stimulant and the most popular drug is one we have all grown to love, cherish and romanticise—coffee.

It is about 5.15 a.m. right now, and I'm drinking a cup of hot black coffee as I type this very statement. And I'm part of a rather large tribe of coffee drinkers. In fact, there are more than a billion people in the world who drink coffee every day. And more than two billion cups of coffee are consumed on a daily basis. We don't just love coffee, we are quite dependent on it. So much so that a ban on coffee for even a single day will probably result in mass riots!

Considering coffee was discovered only a few hundred years ago, why do we love it so much? And what exactly do we love about it? A lot of coffee lovers will say it tastes great and might insist that it's best consumed as is without any milk or sugar. 'Rich', 'deep', 'layered', 'smooth' and, sometimes, 'divine'—these are words black coffee lovers use to describe the taste. Yet, if you had someone try a sip of black coffee for the first time ever, you'd get a very different answer, with the words 'bitter' and 'yuck' definitely featuring somewhere there. So, coffee is not naturally tasty to humans but an acquired taste.

The other thing about coffee is its cool ability to drive away fatigue and lethargy, and bring a certain sprightliness and vigour to the body.

Or, in fewer words, stimulation. Coffee can be a strong stimulant, and this is probably the reason we brought it into our lives back in the 1500s. It wakes us up and keeps us alert in the morning. It gives us a jolt when we feel a slump during the day. It can keep us awake late into the night when we need to stay up. And it can even reduce fatigue and sharpen thinking skills temporarily. No wonder phrases like 'Don't talk to me until I've had my morning coffee' are common.

Caffeine, the component in coffee that is responsible for these effects, is a naturally occurring chemical. It stimulates the central nervous system. While most commonly found in coffee, it is also naturally available in tea, cocoa and, hence, chocolate. But the amount of caffeine is much higher in coffee than in tea or chocolate. In addition to these natural forms, caffeine is also artificially added to other foods like energy drinks.

While there is stimulation, alertness, (acquired) taste and also a solid set of proven health benefits on offer, like most things in life, caffeine is a double-edged sword that we need to learn to use smartly. Because anything that has the power to help so much also has the power to hurt.

> Are you a coffee drinker? How much coffee do you drink per day on average? And how dependant on coffee are you on a daily basis?

#55 Coffee—use it, don't abuse it

Adenosine is a chemical found in our bodies that plays many roles. But it plays a special and significant role in sleep. During the day, every second we are awake, adenosine is secreted and it builds up. When we sleep, adenosine is cleared. Our brains have receptors that track the amount of adenosine in the body at any point of time. When there is more adenosine, you feel sleepy. And when the adenosine is cleared, you don't. When you wake up in the morning after a good night's sleep, you have very little adenosine in the system. Every moment you are awake, more adenosine collects and gets accumulated. By night, there is enough adenosine in your body that needs to be cleared and you feel sleepy.

What caffeine does is interesting. It doesn't neutralise or clear adenosine. It simply blocks the adenosine receptor and tricks the brain into thinking you don't need sleep. This results in a temporary feeling of alertness, which we love. But once the caffeine's effect wears off, the brain is suddenly made aware of the presence of all the adenosine, and you feel sleepy again. This is the reason for the post-coffee crash, where you feel alert soon after drinking coffee, but the lethargy or sleepiness returns after a few hours, sometimes more severely than before.

Also, caffeine has a half-life of five to six hours and so can stay in your system even ten hours post consumption. So, if you had coffee at 5 p.m., you feel its strong stimulant effects within a few minutes. This is when all the caffeine you've consumed is active in your system. While with time, the caffeine will gradually clear from your bloodstream, even at 2 a.m., you will still have some of it. Not enough to keep you alert or active anymore, but enough to affect the quality of your sleep.

Caffeine, though powerful and useful, needs to be consumed carefully because it can very easily become a disruptor for sleep. So, if you are someone struggling with sleep or just trying to improve how easily and how well you're sleeping, here is what you need to do:

- *Have your last coffee 9–10 hours before your bedtime.* If you go to bed at 10 p.m., have your last coffee by noon or 1 p.m. at the latest. If you're a coffee lover and really want that warm, bitter coffee taste later in the day, choose decaf coffee, which is basically coffee with 99.9 per cent of the caffeine removed. It tastes exactly like regular caffeinated coffee but doesn't contain any of the stimulant effects.
- *Stay away from other sources of caffeine in the evening and night.* Energy drinks are the major culprit here, and there are many other reasons to stay away from regularly drinking them. But also keep an eye out for cocoa, tea and colas. You don't have to remove them from your diet, but it helps to be mindful about the quantities.

Caffeine is simply a tool. A tool we have grown very fond of. But, like it is with all other tools, it is on us to find the most effective way to use it.

> Do you have a habit of drinking caffeinated beverages late in the day? And have you noticed how the quality of your sleep changes when you vary the time of caffeine consumption?

#56 Doing the right thing at the wrong time

There are thousands of schools of thought when it comes to fitness, health and well-being. While every single one of them is unique in its own way, there is a small list of actions that all of them will agree have only positive consequences. Exercising is definitely on top of that little list.

While there is nothing wrong with everyone agreeing on this count, there is a small footnote that we must not forget to read: 'Don't do it too close to bedtime.'

Exercise is a wonderful tool for health and fitness. We know this. In fact, exercise is the most effective tool against all causes of mortality. But exercise is highly stimulating. From a physical, mental and hormonal perspective, exercise gets us all revved up—our heart beats faster, breathing rate increases, blood pressure spikes, muscles demand and take up more oxygen, fat is oxidised, body temperature rises, sweating increases, metabolism speeds up and a whole host of hormones are secreted. Even after we stop exercising, it takes anywhere from a few dozen minutes to a few hours for the body to calm down and get to a state of relaxed functioning.

Now, this is a good thing. A great thing, in fact. Because this enables us to use up excess stored energy (fat), build muscle, gain strength and help improve the functionality of our organs and systems. But, when you exercise too close to bedtime, all this stimulation ends up negatively impacting your sleep. And hence your recovery and your health.

As discussed earlier, reducing stimulation at night is important for sleep latency (the time it takes you to fall asleep) and sleep quality. Just like viewing blue light late at night, exercising intensely late in the evening or at night stimulates the brain. This is something we need to avoid.

If you find that the evening is the only time you can exercise and it doesn't affect your sleep, continue doing what you're doing. But if you are someone who exercises in the evening or night and has sleep-related concerns, it would do you a world of good to change your exercise timing to earlier in the day or at least earlier in the afternoon. While a walk after dinner is absolutely fine, do stay away from doing anything physically exerting or exhausting later in the day.

> When is your preferred time to exercise? Have you observed a difference in how easily you fall asleep and how well you sleep based on when you exercise?

#57 Not too late, not too much

Don't you hate it when someone dumps a load of work on you just when you're about to wind down for the day? Well, your body does too.

Our bodies have clear job descriptions. They wear different hats, perform many functions and have many responsibilities that they need to execute in order to keep us alive, well and active. And, incredibly, our bodies are capable of performing at a high level and satisfying all these roles and responsibilities. But only if we cooperate.

In fact, our overall health is the result of a partnership between the conscious—our feelings, thoughts and associated actions and behaviours—and the subconscious, that is, processes and functions that happen without our control and explicit commands. If we can understand what is optimal for our bodies and work with our conscious and subconscious selves, we will be able to achieve better health and quality of life. But if we disregard it and let the conscious work against the subconscious, we're in for a bit of a bumpy ride.

Digestion is one of those processes that the body executes without your conscious awareness. If you think about it, you (the conscious) are in the driver's seat when it comes to deciding when to eat, what to eat, how much to eat, how many times to chew and how slowly or quickly to eat. But once you swallow, you are not in control of the subsequent steps in the process of digestion. Your body takes over and does what needs to be done. The process of energy and nutrient consumption too is a partnership between the conscious (eating) and the subconscious (digesting).

At night, when you're sleeping, your body would really prefer having as little work as possible. This is when it gets to slow down functions, organise memory and focus on recovery. Ideally, it would like to not deal with any of its 'daytime tasks', such as digestion. But, if you eat a huge meal close to bedtime, you're essentially dumping a load of work on your body just before EOD and forcing it to work overtime.

Unfortunately, your body doesn't have a say. So it silently suffers through the extra work like a powerless employee obeying a thoughtless boss. But because it now has to focus on digestion, it isn't able to focus on the tasks necessary for relaxation and restoration. As a result, your sleep is affected. You are unable to fall asleep quickly because your stomach is still full and your body is working quite hard to process all this food. Or you doze off, but have a disturbed night with insufficient deep sleep and you wake up feeling fatigued and unrested.

The one simple change you can make to improve your sleep quality is to eat a light dinner or eat dinner two or three hours before bedtime. I understand this may not be possible for everyone. Dinner is indeed the only meal when most of us eat peacefully and well. So, like with everything else in this book, simply do your best and don't worry about the rest.

> When do you typically eat dinner? Is it your biggest meal of the day? And do you feel that the size of your dinner your sleep?

#58 Get triggered

Imagine yourself at home. It is about 1 p.m., and this is when you usually have lunch. But today, you had breakfast later than usual and you're not as hungry. So you decide to skip lunch and go out for a walk. You put on your shoes, open the door, leave your house and start walking.

But within just a few metres, you smell food. Your neighbours, who probably didn't eat a late breakfast, are getting ready for lunch. And as soon as the smell hits you, your brain starts analysing it. You suddenly (but involuntarily) make sense of the smell and you're able to deduce that it is the aroma of ghee and spices that is in the air. In a few seconds, you're also able to tell which vegetable is being cooked and whether this will be a subtle dish or one loaded with flavour. And in a few more seconds, you start picturing this meal and feeling hungry. And, if the food item being cooked is something you really like, you start to salivate too.

Triggers are fundamental to our existence. It could be food, sleep, sex or drugs—everything starts with a trigger. In fact, one of the basic recommendations when it comes to de-addiction is to remove triggers because that's how powerful they are. Once triggered, the body submits and succumbs to the temptation unless there is a strong conscious opposing force.

But triggers can be manipulated and used to help us or hurt us. For example, placing a pack of cigarettes in front of someone who is trying very hard to quit smoking is adding a trigger to create a negative outcome for the person. But leaving a couple of your favourite books lying around in the living room when you're trying to read more is adding a trigger to create a positive outcome.

Triggers work because a certain type of stimulus (smell, sight, sound, touch, etc.) results in a certain hormone being released. And the hormonal release affects how we feel, which affects how we behave. When it comes to sleep, creating a simple and repeatable bedtime routine serves as a reliable and strong trigger, which signals to the brain that it is time to sleep. This routine is called a 'sleep ritual'.

To take advantage of this simple phenomenon and improve your ease of sleep, here is what you need to do:

- *Sleep and wake up at roughly the same time every day.* You don't have to be anal about it, but make an effort to regularise your sleep times.
- *For 20–30 minutes before bed, do the same things every day.* The only requirement here is that whatever you do, it should be calming and not stimulating. Reading a book, doing some light breathwork for a few minutes and then brushing your teeth before you head to bed is a good example. But this routine can be anything that works for you. The important thing is consistency.

If you can do this, you'll notice that within just a few days, your body will start perceiving this as a signal. And as soon as you open that book (or do whatever the first action in your routine is), you will start feeling sleepy. Falling asleep will become a natural and quick process.

> Chances are you already have a sleep ritual. Think about the last 5–20 minutes of each day. What do you typically do? Does this involve stimulation? What can you add, remove or change to make these 20 minutes a repeatable calm experience?

#59 How much sleep is enough sleep?

From the tiny squirrel to the wondrous elephant, from the croaking frog to the silent snail, every animal needs sleep. While the duration, pattern and timing vary, the basic concept of optimal sleep for repair, growth and rejuvenation applies to all animals, including the supposedly smart, bipedal, diurnal animals called humans.

As human beings, we need different amounts of sleep at different points in our life. As infants, our sleep requirements are rather huge. But as we grow, our sleep requirements decrease with age and plateaus once we become adults. A lot of this is connected to how much work the body is doing and how much growth (creation of new cells) is happening.

Age	Hours required
Under 1	12–16
1–2	11–14
2–5	10–13
6–12	9–12
13–18	8–10
Above 18	7–9

The table reveals two things. First, we need the most sleep when we're born and then the requirement reduces as we approach adulthood. In fact, infants need literally twice the amount of sleep as adults. And second, at every stage, there is not a singular amount of sleep required but a range. How much sleep each person needs varies based on their physiology, stressors and activity levels.

As a general rule for adults, we all need a minimum of 7 hours of sleep for optimal health. While more might be better, it needn't be so for everyone because different people function well with different amounts and patterns of sleep.

You will also need different amounts of sleep at different times. On days when you are working hard physically or mentally, your body will want you to sleep more. Because when more work is done, more recovery is necessary. This is the case when you're ill too—your body needs to recover and so requires you to do less and help recovery by sleeping more.

If you find yourself unusually tired after sleeping the usual amount, look into your past few days. Have you been pushing yourself when training? Have you been working late or thinking about work more than usual? Have you been sleeping a little less lately and has that been piling up? Have you been stressed about something? Or, is there a chance you are catching a cold? Introspect, become aware and give the body what it needs.

> How are you doing when it comes to sleep quantity? On an average, are you close to the 7 hours mark? And, more importantly, do you think more sleep will help you feel better and be more effective in your various roles?

#60 Simplifying sleep

There are smartwatches and smart rings that can track everything from how much sleep you need to how often you move your fingers when sleeping. But the simplest and most effective way to understand if you're sleeping well quantitatively and qualitatively is by tracking how you feel when you wake up.

If you usually wake up fresh and feel energetic and focused through the day without fatigue or periodic sluggishness, your sleep seems to be good for the most part. If not, there is at least one thing you can change or improve that will help.

In this book and out there, there is a lot of information about sleep. And for someone trying to improve their sleep, it can feel like a lot. But it's important to not overthink sleep. Because the more you obsess over sleep, the harder it will be to actually sleep. Because now sleep becomes one more thing to worry about. So, like with everything else but more so than with everything else, simplify.

1. *Try to get a minimum of 7 hours of sleep every night.* Or target 50 hours of cumulative sleep per week. If you are able to get 7+ hours of sleep every night regularly, that's wonderful. If you are unable to because of life's constraints, be it because of your work hours or because you have a little one sleeping with you, don't worry. Do your best and accumulate 50 hours of sleep over the course of the week. This may mean you get more sleep on some

days and less on some other days, and that's OK. With sleep, it is important to realise that we can only work with what we have and we can only do our best to be better.

2. *Naps are fine.* But only as long as they don't affect your night's sleep. That means, napping in the afternoon for about 10–60 minutes to freshen up or make up for a little sleep debt from the previous night is absolutely fine. But make sure this happens earlier in the afternoon and keep it to under an hour. Because napping later in the afternoon or for too long can make it hard for you to sleep well at night, which is the more important part of your total sleep.

3. *Don't let sleep debt build up.* Acute sleep deprivation is common. For innumerable reasons, even the best sleepers sleep less or sleep badly every once in a while. When that happens, you feel the after-effects of physical fatigue and mental sluggishness the next day. A cup of coffee and a few random naps might make you feel better and help you get through the day. But the sleep debt created still exists. As much as possible, repay that debt as quickly as you can by sleeping a little more over the next day or two. Failing to do so will mean that you let the debt add up. Soon it will reach a point where your body's normal functioning drops down a notch below optimal.

4. *Protect yourself against mild but chronic sleep deprivation.* Another way to negatively affect the functional abilities of the body is by sleeping less on a regular basis. This isn't a result of severe sleep deprivation or insomnia, but generally a result of a busy or unstructured lifestyle. When our days are so busy that we don't find enough time to sleep, we suffer the consequences of chronic sleep deprivation. Given how full our days are today, how many tasks we juggle and how much we use devices, way too many people are subjected to these consequences. The way to fix it—prioritise yourself and get to bed on time.

Putting it all together, you are just a few nights away from feeling a lot more energetic, physically stronger and mentally clearer than you are currently feeling. All you need to do is:

- *Step 1*: Prioritise your sleep and give it the importance it deserves.
- *Step 2*: Check how good your sleep latency, quantity and quality are.
- *Step 3*: Make the improvements necessary based on what needs improvement.
- *Step 4*: Be consistent with implementing the improvements.
- *Step 5*: Keep it simple. Don't overthink or get obsessive about sleep.

A good night's sleep may seem elusive. Especially if you are someone who is currently not sleeping well. But remember that you are in control and you are just a few steps away from a superb night's sleep.

> How is your sleep hygiene? What lifestyle changes do you think you need to make? Are you ready to make those changes and improve your sleep quality?

#61 Damage control

Some nights we don't sleep well. This happens to everyone. And it happens for many reasons. Sometimes we know the reasons and sometimes we don't. But bad sleep is a part of every human's life. As long as this happens every once in a while, there is no reason to be worried about it. But you still need to address it and respond to it smartly.

Because a bad night's sleep still takes a toll on the body and makes the following day hard. In fact, a single night of insufficient sleep can cause a perceptible drop in physical performance, impair brain function, increase blood sugar and reduce immune function. It also visibly affects your mood and energy levels, driving you to make suboptimal lifestyle decisions around food and movement.

So, here are four things you can do on the day following a bad night's sleep to reduce the negative consequences and get back on track as quickly as possible.

1. *Eat.* Sleep deprivation is stress on the body. And so is energy deprivation. Don't let them add up. On a day when you haven't had good sleep, realise that you are starting the day in a stressed state. Damage control needs to start from the time you wake up, and eating well is a part of it. So, make sure you eat a nourishing breakfast and continue to eat well throughout the day. Ideally, eat plenty of protein, vegetables and fruits and include starch as

needed. This will combat some of the effects of sleep deprivation by keeping your energy levels up, and also by keeping you from stress eating comfort foods.
2. *Move.* As tempting as it is to skip training, don't. Make it a point to get some form of movement in the morning. Starting your day with some exercise will help you face the day with more energy and in better spirits. But remember that the goal is to energise and not exhaust yourself. So do something light and refreshing. Specifically, don't do anything too hard or risky. This is not the day for that.
3. *Drink your coffee.* If there is a day when you can't do without caffeine, it is such a day. And that's fine. Because this is precisely the time to use this tool. But keep it to the first half of the day. Ideally, have your last coffee (or caffeinated beverage) sometime early in the afternoon. Because caffeine can stay in your system even after 10 hours of consumption, it could disrupt your sleep that night and extend the sleep deprivation to the next day.
4. *Don't nap.* On a day when you are sleep deprived and tired, it's very tempting to take a long nap in the late afternoon or evening. Don't do it. Because that will clear adenosine and make it harder to fall asleep that night, which will make things worse. When you wake up with insufficient sleep, expect that day to be tiring. Especially the second half. Be prepared to push through the day and get to bed earlier than usual. If at all necessary, take a nap of 10–30 minutes in the earlier part of the day.

Remember that bad nights happen and there may not be much you can do about it. What you can do is nip the problem in the bud. Because what is worse than one night of bad sleep is two or more nights of bad sleep. So, if and when you face such a day, respond smartly—do damage control during the day, get to bed early that night and wake up the next day feeling awesome.

> When was the last time you had a bad night's sleep? How did you feel during the day? What did you do to get through the day? Were you able to fix it right away or did the sleep debt continue to build up?

SECTION 5

STRESS

#62 There is no growth without stress

M is a single mom. She works a full-time job and does her best to take care of her seven-year-old. She has some support from her family. But some of them are old and many of them are busy. And they can pitch in only a little. Her life is stressful to say the least. With school drop and pick-up, classes, meal prep, chores, going to work, working late, dealing with a sick child every few weeks and so much more going on in her life, what she wants is a break. But what she really wants is a stress-free life.

N is a tennis player. She depends on the sport and her skill to make a living and build a safe future. She's young and unmarried and has a full day. From waking up well before the sun to giving it her all during practice every day to planning and preparing her meals to managing her finances to doing odd jobs to pay her bills on time, life is stressful. She too wants a stress-free life.

A is an employee at a company and has recently reached middle management. He loves dancing and cooking. But he has to work a job if he wants a fairly comfortable and safe life in a city. So he works all week and spends his weekends learning, dancing, cooking, hosting and, sometimes, even competing. He is happy with his life currently, but still his days are packed throughout the week. And he can't drop anything.

Like M, N and A, billions of people from different walks of life lead stressful lives every single day. And we all do this not because we love it, but because we have to. Because of the promise of a better life in the future. While we all understand why we are stressed and realise at some level that it is necessary, it still stings when things get a little too busy. But we push on. We accept that this is how life is. We drag ourselves through the days of our life, stressed, fatigued and sometimes annoyed and frustrated.

But is this how things are need to be? Is there just no way around this?

Stress is a part of life and always has been. Why we stress has changed over the millennia, but from the early human to you reading this book today, everyone experiences stress and there is no changing that. In fact, stress is the most important ingredient for growth and evolution. It could be a plant or an animal or a single-celled microbe, if there is no stress, there is no evolution. But here is the genius of the design—our bodies and minds are specifically designed to handle stress, and grow stronger with every exposure to stress.

Take the squat, for example. It is an exercise that can make you stronger. But the act of squatting is actually a stressor. And exposing yourself to that stressor and surviving it is what makes you stronger. Consider learning maths or physics. Initially, the concepts involved in these subjects are hard to grasp. Understanding them involves working hard in using our brains, and that is stressful. But it is this stress that enables us to learn by creating synapses, connections and associations in the brain. Or even consider your work. When you start a new role, it feels overwhelming and stressful. But by successfully handling that stressor, soon, your capacity to work increases. This helps you evolve to a point where you are able to do the same amount of work at a much lower stress level.

The thing to keep in mind here is that stress is one of the fundamental aspects of life. Every person, every animal, every plant and every cell undergoes stress. But there's more to stress and we are definitely not doomed to a life of stress and struggle. Because stress, too, is a double-edged sword. We have the power to control it, wield it smartly and use it to our advantage.

> How stressful are your days typically? Would you say you regularly have high stress days? How do you feel on such days? Do you notice a change in discipline and motivation levels on such days?

#63 The two types of stress

Being chased by a dog down the road causes stress. Being chased by a moneylender because you haven't repaid your debt also causes stress. But they are not the same. The first one is what is called 'acute stress', and the second one is called 'chronic stress', and they differ fundamentally in how they affect us physically, mentally and emotionally.

Acute stress is the stress you feel as a direct result of something—a rather drastic physiological and/or psychological reaction to a specific event. It is usually immediate, fairly high in intensity and short lived. Missing a deadline, dropping your favourite chinaware, exercising, getting into an argument with a loved one, rushing somewhere because you're late are all examples of acute stress.

Chronic stress is that stress that builds up over time and doesn't go away easily. It is typically low in intensity but consistent and lingers for a long time. Financial turmoil, demanding jobs, consistent overwork, being stuck in an unhappy marriage, chronic illness are all examples of chronic stress.

The main difference between acute and chronic stress is that, as humans, we are well equipped to handle acute stressors. It is this stress that is part of life, necessary for growth and evolution and makes us stronger. By experiencing the stressor and getting through it, our body and brain learn and prepare us to handle the same or similar stressor better next time. This is why lifting a certain load (stressor) feels hard the first time but gets easier with practice and consistency. This is also why we plan better and leave early if being late the last time caused immense stress. In other words, we experience stress, we learn from the experience and do a tiny bit better next time. So, acute stress is not really a problem.

On the other hand, chronic stress—the sense of feeling overwhelmed, pressured and unhappy for long periods of time—is not something we are equipped to handle. And it is this low grade but consistent stress that is the real problem. The kind that results in anxiety, irritability, stomach ulcers, etc. And if we care about living fit, healthy and happy lives, this one certainly needs to be addressed.

> Think back to the last few weeks and try to become aware of what kind of stress you experience more in your everyday life. If it is acute, how are you handling it? If it is chronic, are you willing to take the necessary steps to address it?

#64 Stop, listen and become aware

The first step towards addressing stress is awareness. Very often, people don't realise they are stressed. Like the famous 'frog in boiling water' story goes, living in chronic stress is like a frog living in water that very gradually gets warmer. At no point does the frog feel a change in temperature drastic enough to jump out. Since the temperature rises very slowly, the frog adapts to its new living conditions by suffering silently and continues to live there until it gets extremely uncomfortable or unliveable. Similarly, a lot of us go through everyday life chronically stressed. Suffering silently.

And this affects our physical, mental and emotional health, leaving us frustrated, anxious, depressed and diseased. In such a scenario, fitness, health and wellness are simply not attainable. Because when we are chronically stressed, we struggle to sleep well. We find it hard to gather the physical energy or mental motivation to exercise. We make suboptimal food choices driven by immediate gratification. And we simply find it impossible to truly focus or prioritise health.

Before we learn how to address this, we need to learn to acknowledge it. There are plenty of questionnaires out there to help you understand if you are stressed or not. But here are three simple questions that will do the job:

1. Have you consistently felt pressured, overwhelmed or anxious in the last few weeks or months?

2. Do you have a sense of 'feeling stuck' or think 'there is no escape' or ask yourself 'when will this end'?
3. Do you find yourself irritable, frustrated or annoyed regularly?

If you answered yes to even one of the three questions, you're dealing with some amount of chronic stress. Addressing it is something you owe to yourself, and it will most certainly help you look, feel and function a lot better.

Addressing chronic stress involves two broad aspects—stress tolerance and stress management. While stress tolerance is about optimising your threshold for stress, stress management is about optimising the quantum of stress in your life. It is important to learn about both of them.

> Are you struggling with chronic stress? If you said yes, remember that you are not alone and this is not unusual. Now that you have acknowledged it, are you willing to take steps to address it?

#65 Tolerance is a skill

There are people who have packed days and multiple stressors in life but still move forward with a smile and a sense of purpose. There are also people who lose their cool and lash out at the smallest inconvenience. People are different. Some people handle stress better than others, and this tolerance is a result of many factors, from life experiences to current life situations.

Stress tolerance is a skill. And like the many skills we've discussed, this skill too is one that each of us possesses at varying levels. More importantly, it is a skill we can consciously work on and improve. With better stress tolerance, we can get through life with fewer bumps, bruises and scratches, which will enable us to feel better in general and live healthier lives.

As a concept, building tolerance to stress is simple and no different from building tolerance to anything. It requires three fundamentals—acknowledgement, exposure, repetition. Let's break this process down into five simple steps.

1. *Identify stress early.* Sounds simple, but this does take some effort. More often than not, we don't realise we are stressed until we see explicit indications of it or feel out of control. Learning to be aware of your feelings and behaviours and identifying right when you are beginning to feel stressed is very important. It gives

you a chance to act on it well ahead of time and well before you reach the point of no return. Early detection is indeed the key.
2. *Call it out.* If you've learnt to identify stress early, the next step is to acknowledge it openly. Telling yourself (or the person or people involved) that you can sense that you are getting stressed is extremely powerful. By acknowledging it and calling it out, you have taken some control of the situation. You will take your next step and say your next words more mindfully.
3. *Don't be afraid of it.* Once you've acknowledged that you are stressed, be brave about it. Understand that it is OK to be stressed, and face the stressor. Remind yourself that the goal now is not to run away from stress but to regulate and manage it.
4. *Think, don't worry.* At times, chronic lifestyle stress can feel overwhelming. During such times, choose 'how' instead of 'why'. When thinking about your next step, ask yourself, 'How can I make the situation better for myself?' as opposed to 'Why is this happening to me?' This will enable you to view the situation from a position of control and prevent you from feeling helpless.
5. *Do a tiny bit better next time.* One thing you can be sure of is that you will get enough chances to be stressed in life and, hence, get enough opportunities to learn how to handle it. Use this to your advantage. Increasing your stress tolerance is a process that requires repetition and practice. So every time you find yourself feeling stressed, try to learn from the experience and do a tiny bit better.

Like strength or endurance, stress tolerance is built by repeatedly exposing ourselves to stressors. While it seems counterintuitive to do so, remember that stress will always be something you need to deal with. So make a conscious effort to deal with it a little better every time.

> Given that there are people with a whole range of stress tolerance, what do you think your tolerance levels are? Can you tolerate high stress and handle stressful situations calmly or do you struggle with stress? Can you think of one other person who is the opposite of you in this regard?

#66 Is there good and bad stress?

How sweet do you like your cake? How hot would you like the sauna? How loud do you like the TV? How much salsa would you like on your burrito? Different people will have different answers, but everyone will agree to the universal answer—not too much, not too little. Just right.

The Goldilocks principle says that humans tend to prefer everything in the 'just right' zone. Challenges that are just hard enough are preferred over challenges that are too hard or too easy. Food that is too salty or insufficiently salted is not liked as much as food that is salted just right. Economic growth that is too fast or too slow is harder to cope with than moderate growth. This simply means we tend to prefer things in the optimal zone and not in the maximal or minimal zone. And this is very true when it comes to stress too.

There is a certain amount of stress that each of us can handle well and thrive while doing it. If the stress level goes any higher, we struggle to cope, and if it is lower, then we get lethargic. This is the difference between eustress and distress. Eustress is a positive form of stress in a manageable amount that has a beneficial effect on health, motivation, performance and emotional well-being. And distress, or negative stress, is the opposite of that.

The point of stress management is stress regulation with the goal of optimisation rather than reduction. While stress regulation might mean reducing stress levels for many, there certainly are people who may need more stress than they currently experience in order to feel their best. And one thing to remember here is that we are operating at a relative scale and not an absolute one. So how much stress is optimal will vary from person to person based on their stress tolerance capabilities and their stress threshold.

So there is in fact good and bad stress. The good stuff is what brings the best out of us and the bad stuff is what brings out the worst. But this depends on the nature of the stressor, the quantum, the reason behind it and, most importantly, the mindset with which we approach it.

> Do you have stressors in your life that bring out a better version of you? Do you prefer working in slightly stressful situations? Can you think of a scenario, role or situation where this is true?

#67 Stress management 101

Managing stress is a lot like playing Tetris. The main idea is to keep playing the game without letting it all build up. And, like Tetris, we need to be strategic, patient and, at times, agile. Here are six simple tips that will help you manage your stress levels on a daily basis.

1. *Prioritise*. The simplest and most common reason for high stress is doing too much. Understanding that we can't do everything for everyone all the time and prioritising the right things is important. What are the actions, people and tasks that are most important in your life? Most of your time, energy and attention should be directed towards these. To be able to do this, you will need to learn to say no more often and be OK with it. Being clear about your priorities will make this a lot easier.
2. *Enough is enough*. The problem with more is that more is never enough. When we seek more and we achieve it, our logical next step is to want even more. This is a process that is never ending and never satisfying. Understanding enough is enough is a mindset that will help calm you and view things differently. Because enough doesn't mean settling for less. Enough means being happy with what you have today while being aware that more will come your way tomorrow.
3. *Be bored*. Being constantly stimulated is another reason why we are constantly stressed. We allow ourselves to be bombarded by some stimulus or the other. We hardly give our brains a chance to be free and our minds a chance to be still. So much that being

bored is one of the hardest things to deal with today. While not as fun as being stimulated, it is OK to be bored. Try it. Good things will come from it.

4. *Take mini-breaks.* It's obvious that we all need sufficient breaks to rest, recover and come back stronger. Yet millions every year work, push and hustle for months together without resting or de-stressing. While the idea is to accumulate holidays for a longer vacation, this is leading to a vicious cycle—work hard → burnout → big reset → work hard → burnout. While this cycle, with its giant ups and downs, might seem like the norm, it is detrimental to our physical and mental well-being, to say the least.

5. *Do the wellness basics.* When it comes to wellness, the basics are breathing, walking and connecting. Take time to do simple breathwork that enables you to breathe slowly, deeply and consciously. Walk in nature and give your body and mind a break from the stressors of everyday life. And connect with people either through family, community or activity. The basics might seem boring. But they work wonders and work every time.

6. *Take control.* Irrespective of what happens, take ownership of your actions and accountability for your behaviour. While this might feel like a tough thing to do at first, once you get into the habit of viewing things from this perspective, you will feel more in control and less like a victim.

Chronic stress can be hard to live with. But once you understand that stress is a necessary part of life and your task is simply to optimise the type and quantum of stress and actively work on managing it, things will feel a lot better.

> How do you think you are currently managing stress? Which one of these six actions do you think will make a big difference to your stress levels and life?

#68 Breathe your way to better health

There is so much talk about hacking health and finding fast, optimal ways to improve quality of life. In fact, we all seem to really like the pills, potions and procedures that can help us calm down, manage stress and sleep better. But the truth is that the most effective method to do all this was invented thousands of years ago, and it is a secret that has been hidden in plain sight. And unlike most things in fitness that are simple but not easy, this one is actually simple AND easy.

Breathwork or pranayama is the regulation of breath through certain techniques and exercises. Depending on the technique, pranayama can have a range of benefits, from improved lung function to better sleep to stress and anxiety management. It's not hard to learn or practise. And it is definitely not something that only a select few can do. Breathwork is something that can be done by anyone, and it guarantees improvements in mental and physical wellness. The only requirement—you need to do it regularly.

While there are many different types of breathwork and more techniques are being experimented with and invented every day, here are the fundamentals about breathwork that you need to be aware of:

- You are not in control of how fast your heart beats and how quickly your mind races. But you are in control of your breathing. And by

consciously slowing down your breathing and controlling it, you can gradually get your mind, heart and the rest of your body to listen to you and follow your pace.
- *Breathing directly affects how much oxygen your cells get.* When you deepen and slow down your breathing from the usual shallow pattern, you allow more oxygen to enter each cell, thus allowing better communication between cells.
- *Deep and slow breathing also causes changes in hormone secretion patterns.* Depending on the breathing technique used, you can expect improved alertness, higher energy during the day, better focus, reduced stress, better recovery, reduced anxiety/depression and even an overall sense of happiness and well-being.

How do you take advantage of this simple but incredible technique and improve the quality of your life?

- *Spend 5–20 minutes every day doing breathwork.* If you can find a slot to do this regularly every day, great. If not, don't worry about it. Do it whenever you can.
- *If you're a beginner, don't worry about finding the best technique or setting up a space that is quiet and perfect.* Simply sit down, close your eyes and breathe slowly and deeply. It's OK if there are thoughts and distractions. Just try not to get attached to a thought or frustrated by distractions. Let them come and, more importantly, let them go.
- *Don't expect yourself to be in a meditative state or in any way perfect* (like you'd imagine experts and saints would be). Instead, have no expectations. Sit, breathe and slow down. That's it.

Of the many types of breathwork available today, here are four very simple techniques I highly recommend with sleep, stress management and recovery in mind.

1. *Morning*: Breathe in for 4 seconds through your nose and breathe out quickly (but completely) through your mouth. Do this for 5–20 minutes every morning within an hour of waking up. This will stimulate your sympathetic nervous system and help you feel awake and alert.
2. *Evening*: Breathe in for 4 seconds through your nose and breathe out for 8 seconds through your nose or mouth. Do this for 5–20 minutes every evening within 1–2 hours of your bedtime. This will stimulate your parasympathetic nervous system and help you feel relaxed and sleepy.
3. *Stress reduction*: If and when you feel overwhelmed, do 'cyclic sighing' for 2–5 minutes. A cyclic sigh involves taking a deep breath in through your nose to a point where your lungs are about 80 per cent full, then adding a second 'sip' of air through your nose (trying to get to 100 per cent fullness), and then exhaling slowly with a sighing sound through your mouth. A few minutes of this will reduce anxiety, slow your heart rate, increase serotonin secretion and make you feel more relaxed and clear. Use this drill as a tool to reduce stress whenever necessary.
4. *Lung capacity improvement*: Set a 20-minute timer. Lie down with your belly facing up. Breathe in through your nose and out through your mouth or nose. For the first breath, spend 1 second to breathe in and 1 second to breathe out. For the second breath, 2 seconds in and 2 seconds out. And so on for as high as you can make it. Once you get to a point of comfortable maximum (where you are breathing comfortably but you can't go any higher), stick to that tempo for the remainder of the time. On the first day, you may not get too high. Most people will max out in the fourth to eighth rung on day one. But with a couple of weeks of practice, you'll find that your lung capacity improves and you are able to go much higher. This requires a little more time than the other three drills, but it will improve your lung capacity significantly

and will have benefits that apply to both everyday life and to high-intensity fitness based activities.

Simple can be powerful. And breathwork is proof that just a few minutes of relaxation and breathing every day can have a significantly positive impact on your life. But, as always, remember that these drills, like all the knowledge, facts and frameworks in this book, are all simple tools. Tools that are now at your disposal. Use what you need based on your current goals and circumstances and save the rest for later. Because this journey of betterment is long and you will most certainly need a loaded toolkit in order to keep going.

> What do you think about breathwork? Do you do it or is it not your cup of tea? Now that you know how easy it is and how effective it can be, would you like to give one of these a shot today? Could you maybe close your eyes for 2 minutes right now and try breathing slowly and deeply?

SECTION 6

WEIGHT LOSS

#69 We all care about how we look, and there's nothing wrong with that

Many years ago, when I first started working on myself, my primary goal was weight loss. I was overweight, unhealthy and unfit. More specifically, I weighed about 20 kilos above my ideal weight, with scary blood sugar numbers and lipid profile. Also, I couldn't run more than a few metres without getting an asthma attack. All this at the ripe old age of twenty-five. As much as this came as a rude shock to me, it wasn't uncommon then and is certainly not uncommon now.

To be completely honest, as I think back, the health and fitness issues were more of a concern than my weight was. My fitness levels were so bad that I would have breathing difficulty within just a couple of minutes of any activity, and this was affecting the quality of my life to the point where I played no sports and did nothing active. My cholesterol levels were so bad that had I not addressed it immediately, I'd have been prescribed statins. And that would have been the start of a different journey—one that would have involved a lot more pill popping and a lot less of lifting weights. But, somehow, the need to reduce my weight was larger than addressing these.

I'm sure I'm not alone here, and a lot of you can relate to this feeling. In fact, back in 2012, I was working with a client who wanted to lose weight. She was fairly young, stood 5' 2" tall, was not very active and made suboptimal nutrition choices. As a result, her body weight had reached an all-time high of 84 kilos. Going through her blood work, it was clear that while weight gain was one of the side effects of her lifestyle, there were others too. Specifically, her fasting blood sugar was 235 mg/dL. Ideally, we want this number to be between 70 and 100 mg/dL. I designed a plan for her and she worked on it. While it involved nutrition and exercise, it focused more on nutrition since that's what was needed immediately.

After four weeks, during our review, she expressed her dissatisfaction with the programme. She said she had been putting in a lot of work in changing her nutrition habits, but her results were not satisfactory. Her body weight had reduced by 2.5 kilos. A lot of you reading this may also feel like that isn't much (and we'll discuss the optimal rate of weight loss soon) but there's more to the story.

While she was focused on the scale and how her body weight changed, what she didn't even notice was her blood sugar. It had dropped from 235 mg/dL to 118 mg/dL in just four weeks, without any medication. I brought this up to her attention. While she was happy to note that, she remained dissatisfied. The scale weight hadn't moved as much as she had wanted it to, and that's all she cared about. And that's OK.

It's hard to understand or explain this, but body weight (and how we look) matters a lot to us. Even more than health, functionality or performance. This may be because of the media pushing unattainable body sizes and shapes as the norm or maybe because we care more about what we (and others) can see more than how we feel. But most of us want to look better and there's absolutely nothing wrong with that. We just need to ensure we do it smartly because what we really want is to be lean and strong, not skinny and weak.

> How much does your aesthetic progress matter to you when it comes to fitness? Is weight loss, looking lean, being muscular or just somehow looking better your primary goal? Or are you considering weight loss as a welcome side effect of better health? There are no right and wrong answers here. But it is very important that you are aware of what your real goal is and be clear about it.

#70 Your body doesn't want you to lose weight

I'm sure you'll agree that everyone is in a hurry to lose weight. Every diet and gym advertises rapid weight loss, and every nutrition expert is trying to figure out ways to increase the rate of weight loss. Because everyone wants to lose weight as quickly as possible. But have you wondered why that is?

Because weight loss is uncomfortable. Eating less, saying no to delicious things, suffering through endurance exercise, lifting weights, learning new movements and trying to be disciplined are all uncomfortable. And since we are designed to avoid discomfort, we want this uncomfortable process to be over as quickly as possible. It's like walking barefoot on a hot day and going from one shaded area to another. You don't really want to linger on the hot ground. You want to get to the other side as quickly as you can.

For your body too, losing weight is not comfortable. Weight loss is a significant event. During weight loss, all the organs and systems in your body, including your heart, lungs, muscles, bones, hormones, blood flow, breathing rate, blood composition, glucose levels and triglycerides, are affected. And rapid weight loss means that these organs and systems need to be pushed to the very extreme—to mobilise stored energy (fat) out of cells and then oxidise it. This is not something the body does readily because of the intensity of work involved. Also, fat is energy that is stored by the body for future use.

Like money you have invested for the future. So, naturally, accessing this stored energy and using it is not something the body is very open to. And it's not going to make it easy for you to do it. This too is a survival mechanism.

Ideally, your body doesn't want you to lose weight. Because losing weight means loss of water and tissue. And a gradual reduction in energy and matter in an animal signals atrophy, which happens in nature only when there isn't enough food, which is a red flag. Or when the animal is diseased, which is also a red flag. Or when the animal is old and is winding down, which is the ultimate red flag.

So, when you force your body to lose weight, and do so at a high rate, it goes into panic mode. With red lights and alarms going off everywhere, your body, in an effort to keep you from dying, brings about physiological changes that slow down this process of losing energy and matter (weight loss). You hate it and you want the process to happen quickly so that you can look better and feel lighter. So, you keep pushing and doing your thing. Your body, on the other hand, doesn't get today's aesthetic demands. It wants you alive, fat or fit. And so it resists and does its thing. As a result, you are caught in this see-saw phase with your body where you both want different things. It sucks, but it's necessary to see-saw. Because that's the only way to make sure you don't go too far on either side.

> Let's say there is a way to lose 15 kilos overnight. Would that be a good thing? Of course, you can wake up tomorrow morning looking amazing. But can you imagine how much stress every system, organ and cell in your body has to go through to make this happen? And, what do you think would happen if someone did this five nights in a row?

#71 What you really want is 'fat loss'

Let's say you're going on a long trek. You're carrying a backpack with a few things in it. You have water, food, books to read, books to write, some rocks you picked up along the way, a phone charger and some knick-knacks you bought at a sale. All is well and you're enjoying the trek with its incredible views, steep slopes and tree cover. In a few hours, you start feeling tired. Gradually, you find it harder to move forward with each step. You slow down and take more breaks, but it still feels hard. Your guide says your bag is what is weighing you down and the only way to make the rest of the trek is to lighten the load. What are you going to dump and what are you going to keep? There are items in your backpack that are essential and then there are items that are non-essential for the trek. Will you throw away the water? Or the knick-knacks? Will you keep the rocks? Or the charger? What do you need more right now—the books or the food? Surely, you'll retain the things that are essential for you to complete the trek and toss out the ones that are not.

This is the difference between weight loss and fat loss.

Weight loss is a blanket term and is about reducing the weight of your body. That's it. It doesn't matter what contributes to this weight loss. You can lose water or fat or muscle or even chop off a couple of limbs, and it will still qualify as weight loss. It's like reducing the weight of your backpack by randomly reaching into it, grabbing whatever you touch and throwing that thing away without paying attention to what it is. There is no differentiation between what is essential and non-essential.

But fat loss is a specific term. It's about losing fat, and only fat, from your body. That means that while the goal of weight loss is to somehow reduce weight, the goal of fat loss is to reduce weight by reducing specifically the amount of fat you have in your body without losing muscle mass and strength.

If you are someone who is currently overweight, it simply means you have accumulated extra energy and stored it as fat, which is what you want to lose. Even though you may want 'weight loss', what you really want is 'fat loss', because I'm fairly certain that you don't want to lose muscle, bone or parts of your body. But if you can strike the right balance between movement, nutrition and sleep, you can rest assured that you will lose fat and maintain muscle and bone mass. In short, you'll lose weight in a healthy and happy manner.

> What do you really want to lose? Is it just the number on the scale that you are concerned about? Or are you looking to lose fat from specific parts of your body?

#72 The first law of thermodynamics

A lot of us use the common word 'energy' in everyday communication. But what exactly is energy?

Energy is the capacity to do work. And in order for us to do *any* work, we need energy. Work here refers to anything we do. From exercising to sitting and watching TV to sleeping to doing absolutely nothing except breathing, it is all work. In fact, we need energy to be alive even if we are comatose. Because the beating of the heart needs energy. So does respiration, blood circulation and everything else necessary to stay alive.

Energy exists in many forms—electrical energy, heat energy, wind energy, sound energy, atomic energy and so on. And here is a very interesting thing—energy can neither be created nor destroyed. It can only be transferred from one form to another. This is Einstein's first law of thermodynamics. Practically, this means that we can gain energy from other energy sources, and we can convert our energy into other types of energy. But we simply cannot produce new energy or destroy existing energy. For example, we get energy through food. When we eat, the energy that exists in food is transferred to us. We then use that energy to do work, and the work we do produces a different form of energy and so on.

Let's say you eat two bananas. The energy from the bananas is transferred to you. Now you use that food energy to push the pedals of a bicycle. The cycle's tyres spin and create mechanical energy. A dynamo is attached to the tyre of the bicycle. The dynamo converts this mechanical energy from the spinning cycle wheel into electrical energy. This electrical energy lights up a bulb that is on the front of the cycle. This produces light energy, which enables you to see at night. This light energy ensures you do not crash into a tree. While there seems to be no apparent connection between eating bananas and not crashing into a tree, in this example, it is the energy from the banana that's actually keeping you safe.

In the larger sense, what the first law of thermodynamics really means is that we can't create something from nothing, and we can't convert something into nothing. Practically, this means we cannot gain weight unless we consume more energy than necessary, and we can't lose weight unless we convert existing energy in the body into some other form of energy.

> Have you felt like you're not losing weight even though you are eating less? With the first law of thermodynamics in mind, do you feel it's possible to consume less food (energy) than you need but still not lose weight? Or is there a chance that you think you are consuming less energy but you're actually consuming as much energy as your body needs to maintain weight and hence are not losing weight?

#73 Calories in, calories out

Calorie, probably one of the most commonly used words in the twenty-first century, is nothing but a unit of energy. Like how metre is one of the units of length and gram that of mass, calorie is one of the units used to quantify energy. While calorie is what we use casually, the actual unit is kilocalorie, or kcal. So, when you say a normal adult needs about 2,000 calories a day, you mean to say the adult needs 2,000 kcal worth of energy every day. And when you say a slice of cake has 300 calories and an apple has only 100 calories, what you're saying is that the slice of cake can provide us with 300 kcal worth of energy, which is three times the energy we can procure from an apple.

In order to function optimally, we all need a certain amount of energy. We measure this in kcal. And we need to procure this energy by eating other things that contain energy—what we call food. This energy in food is stored in the form of macronutrients—protein, carbohydrates and fats. As a part of digestion, our bodies break these macronutrients down and extract energy from them. Every gram of protein and carbohydrate provides us with 4 kcal worth of energy each, and every gram of fat provides us with 9 kcal worth of energy. This is why fatty foods are considered dense in calories—because they can store and provide us with more energy. Once extracted, the energy is either used by the body immediately or stored in specialised cells (fat cells) so that we can use them later based on need. Since everything from moving to working to staying alive requires us to spend energy, we need a constant supply of energy coming in. But thanks to evolution and our body's ability to store energy, we don't have to eat constantly.

One other thing to keep in mind is that consumption is not absorption. Since we consume energy stored in the form of macronutrients in food and then break it down to extract energy, the amount of energy we consume and the amount of energy our bodies absorb are not always the same. Because the process of breaking down food into energy and nutrients requires energy for the process itself.

How is all this connected to body weight and weight loss? All of us are made up of cells. We have trillions of them. Each cell is made up of molecules, which are made up of basic elements such as carbon, oxygen, hydrogen and nitrogen, which are made from energy. So, essentially, we are all devices that procure, store and convert energy into other forms of energy and manufacture matter.

If the amount of energy we absorb from food and the amount of energy we expend through living are the same, our body weight remains the same. We call this weight maintenance.

If the amount of energy we absorb from food is *more* than the amount of energy we expend through living, the excess energy is stored in cells in the form of fat or used to build more bone and muscle, and our body weight increases. We call this weight gain.

If the amount of energy we absorb from food is *less* than the amount of energy we expend through living, then we burn matter (stored fat, glycogen and muscle), convert it into energy and use up this internal energy to make up for the difference, and our body weight decreases. We call this weight loss.

This, in essence, is how body weight change happens and this is what people mean when they say, 'It all comes down to calories in and calories out.'

> How does understanding energy and its conversion to different forms change your understanding of weight loss? Are you able to accept that a lack of change in body weight is simply because there is no energy surplus or shortage?

#74 In a world of abundance, a shortage is what we need

Irrespective of who you are, where you live, your origin, your sex, your gender, what you eat and what you do for a living, this universal equation applies to you because it applies to every animal:

Energy expended−Energy absorbed = Net energy used

That means that when the energy expended by the body is more than the energy absorbed, a shortage in energy occurs. That shortage is addressed by using up energy that was previously stored in the body. If this equation seems unfamiliar, here's the same equation in a more recognisable form:

Calories out−Calories in = Calorie deficit

When people say 'calories out', they mean the amount of energy (measured in kcal) used up by the body. And when they say 'calories in', they mean not the amount of energy consumed, but the amount of energy the body has absorbed out of the energy that is consumed. And that means, if you want to reduce the weight of your body, you need to create a 'calorie deficit', which means you need to ensure that there is a shortage of energy by ensuring that the amount of energy *flowing out* of the body is higher than the amount of energy *flowing into* the body.

The factors that affect 'calories out' are basal metabolic rate (BMR), non-purposeful movement (NPM), activities of daily life (ADL) and exercise.

Basal metabolic rate is the amount of energy required to simply keep a person alive. If you did literally nothing except be alive and breathe (like you're comatose), how much energy would you use up? This is your BMR. It varies a lot from person to person and is dependent on four things: genetic make-up, body weight, body composition and activity levels. People who are heavy have a higher BMR (compared with those who are lighter) simply because a bigger body means more cells and more cells need more energy. People who have more muscle mass have a higher BMR because muscle is harder to maintain and more 'expensive' to feed for the body. This is why two people at the same body weight but different body composition (ratio of muscle, fat, bone and water in the body) can have very different BMRs. And people who are more active have a higher BMR because more activity means more recovery, and that requires more energy.

Non-purposeful movement includes all the little movements we do without much thought. Fidgeting, facial expressions, scratching our head, tapping our feet and blinking are some examples. Each of these actions, as small as they are, need energy, and when considered over the course of days, weeks and years, they do add up.

Activities of daily life include essentially everything we do in a day outside of exercise, sports and any other activity aimed at physical fitness. Walking, climbing stairs, bathing, cleaning the house, procuring groceries, typing, writing, shopping and going to the movies are all examples.

And exercise, well, is any activity we do specifically aimed at health, fitness or performance.

So, energy outflow or 'calories out' = BMR + NPM + ADL + Exercise.

When it comes to energy inflow or 'calories in', there is only one factor and that is food. In other words, we have only one natural way of procuring energy and that is by eating.

In order to lose weight, we need to create a calorie deficit. And for that we need to do two seemingly simple things—increase the total energy outflow and decrease the total energy inflow.

> If you had to create a calorie deficit, given your current life situation, preferences and constraints, what are two things you would do to increase your energy outflow? And what are two changes you would make to decrease the total energy inflow?

#75 Move more, do more, burn more

How many calories will I burn from strength training? Which exercise burns the most calories? Why has my metabolism slowed down? What should I do to burn off that milkshake I had this morning?

These are all common questions today from anyone who is looking to lose weight. And the reason they are asking these questions is because they are trying to do the first seemingly simple thing—increase the total energy outflow. But, before we get to understanding how, let's understand something very important.

Even though 'calories out' = BMR + NPM + ADL + Exercise, all four factors do not contribute equally to energy outflow. Usually, your BMR accounts for about 60–75 per cent of total energy outflow. That's massive! And depending on what each person's everyday life is like (ranging from sedentary to extremely active), the remaining 25–40 per cent of energy is expended through a combination of different types of movement.

Broadly, the two ways of increasing energy outflow (or burning more calories) are to increase movement and increase BMR.

Increasing movement is simple, and here is how you can make it sustainable.

- *Focus on ADL.* While we think of exercise as the main channel for burning calories, increasing activity during the day could have a larger effect. This is mainly because we have more time for ADL than we do for exercise. By smartly increasing how much and how often we move throughout the day, we can make a significant difference. While ADL includes all forms of movement, for most of us today, walking is the most accessible way to harness the power of ADL. As you know, we have arrived at a place of convenience where we don't have the need to walk anymore. But in order to increase energy outflow, we need to move more. So, walk, walk a lot, walk often and walk for no reason. For every 1,000 steps you take, you burn about 25–50 calories, depending on your body weight and speed. If you can manage to walk 7,000–15,000 steps per day, you can burn anywhere from 200 to 600 calories. Do remember that these steps need not be done in one shot. In other words, you don't have to set aside 2 hours just for walking. Instead, strategise and walk more during your day. Walk when you take phone calls, walk to the store, take the stairs, walk the dog, take the trash out, go for a 10-minute walk before and after lunch and use every opportunity you get to walk.

- *Exercise regularly.* Don't overthink this. There are many, many types of exercise, and each form of exercise has a different effect on the body. Some help expend more energy, some help build muscles and bones, some make you mobile and some do it all. The specifics don't quite matter yet. For now, just make sure you are exercising regularly. Ideally, you want to get to a point where you are doing some form of exercise on five to six days of the week and are expending about 2,000–3,000 kcal every week from exercise (roughly 300–600 kcal per session of exercise). That said, start wherever you are right now. Maybe you are only walking 3,000 steps a day and exercising two days a week. That's fine. It's a great place to start. Next week, try to increase your steps to 4,000 and exercise to three days. Do that for a couple of weeks and then make it 5,000 steps and four days of exercise and so on.

The most important thing with activity and exercise is this—you need to want to make it happen. When you look at what you need to do and change, it could feel overwhelming. But once you stop asking yourself 'Can I do this?' and start asking yourself 'How can I do this?', you will come up with strategies and solutions. It all comes down to intent. If you have it, you will most certainly find a way to make it happen.

> What is your ADL like today? Do you do a lot of manual labour or walking? If not, how can you bring in more activity during your day?
>
> What is your exercise frequency and intensity today? Do you know roughly how many calories you burn from exercise every week? Do you need to increase it? If yes, how would you do that?

#76 Build more muscle, burn more calories

Here is a task for you—earn 50 per cent more this month than what you earned last month. But you have to do it without quitting your job and have to sustain this 50 per cent increase for the next many years. How would you go about it?

The fastest way to do this is to work more. You might work overtime or work weekends or take up a few new projects. This will result in an immediate increase in your income, and that's great in the short term. But, if you need to sustain this in the long term, you'll need to work nights and weekends for years, and that isn't sustainable. The smarter way to do it is to figure out a way to do your job better. Get promoted or find a better-paying role or, if you're an entrepreneur or content creator, improve your product or service and sell more or sell it for more. This way, you will earn more from the same working hours as before. This means you've found a way to increase your value per hour, which is certainly the better long-term approach for growth.

Increasing your BMR is just like that.

Increasing energy outflow through movement (exercise and ADL) is like working more hours. You can do it, but only to a certain extent, after which it becomes unsustainable. Increasing your BMR is like getting a promotion or bettering your product or service. It's the smartest way to burn more calories through the day without having to increase the amount of time you're exercising or moving.

'Metabolism' essentially refers to all the physical and chemical processes in the body that produce, convert or use energy. So having a higher metabolism or higher metabolic rate means more energy conversion and usage, which means more energy outflow.

As mentioned before, BMR depends on four aspects. But we can control only two of those. We have no control over our genetics and body size (height, organ size, bone structure, etc.). But we have control of our body composition and activity levels. And improving your body composition, by increasing muscle mass and reducing fat mass, is a smart and guaranteed way of increasing BMR. Because building muscle and maintaining muscle are two expensive processes that require the body to spend a lot of energy. In fact, if you can find a way to build more muscle and maintain it, you will force your body to burn more calories even when you're at rest, which is what increasing your BMR means.

And luckily for you, there is a simple way to do this—strength train two to four times a week, and do this consistently. That's it. When you do this, you give your body a reason to maintain the existing muscle mass and also build new muscle over a period of time. This will slowly but surely increase your BMR, which will result in increasing your overall energy outflow in the long term.

> Are you actively working on building for the future? Do you strength train regularly with the intention of increasing or maintaining muscle mass? If yes, are you doing it consistently? If not, what is stopping you from making it a consistent part of your life?

#77 A very short summary of how to burn more calories

As tempting as it is to complicate things, you don't have to. Keep it simple, and do the following if you want to consistently increase energy outflow and create a sustainable calorie deficit.

- *Exercise*: Do some form of exercise every week and target burning about 2,000–3,000 calories per week from exercise. This can be through anything. You can walk, run, dance, play sports, lift weights, go kayaking, cycle, swim or do any activity you please. Your goal, from a calorie burning perspective, is to accumulate enough activity through the week to burn the required amount of energy. This means you can do this as three days of exercise burning 700–1,000 kcal on each day, or split it up across all seven days and burn 300–400 kcal per day.
- *Strength train*: Since strength training is what will build muscle and increase your BMR, ensure you strength train at least two days every week. It doesn't matter which equipment you use, what your specific training plan is and what set-rep template you choose. But it definitely matters that you load your muscles and work on them regularly every week.
- *Walk*: Get in 10,000–15,000 steps every day. It's OK if you are nowhere close to this right now. Start where you are. Slowly, every week, increase the total number of steps per day by 500 or 1,000. And soon you'll find yourself at this level of activity.

That's it. These three actions will take care of increasing energy expenditure in the short term and also lay the foundation for increased energy expenditure in the long term by increasing your BMR. If you can do these regularly, you can certainly set yourself up for long-term success in weight loss and management.

> Can you exercise, do strength training and walk—and do these three things consistently? More importantly, *how* can you make them a regular part of your life? What changes do you need to make in your day and life to remain committed to these three actions?

#78 Restrict yourself, mindfully and consistently

There are three fundamental ways to save money:
1. You can earn more money while maintaining your current expenses.
2. You can earn the same amount of money but reduce your current expenses.
3. You can earn more money and reduce your expenses.

Of these, the third option is clearly the way to save the most money because you are working on both ends—the inflow and outflow.

Creating a calorie deficit and losing weight is similar. You have three fundamental ways to do it:
1. Increase energy outflow while maintaining your current energy inflow.
2. Maintain the same energy outflow but reduce your energy inflow.
3. Increase energy outflow and reduce energy inflow.

In the previous chapters, we've learnt how to work on the energy outflow. But that's not enough. Because once you increase energy outflow, your body will automatically, and subconsciously, increase energy inflow.

Why? Because when the body does more work, the organs, muscles, bones and all associated cells demand more nutrients and energy to maintain homeostasis. As a result, appetite goes up, calorie-dense foods appear tastier, and you end up with more energy inflow, even without your knowledge. So, if you're only focusing on increasing energy outflow, even though you feel like you're eating the same foods as before, you will end up unintentionally eating more food. This will help the body achieve homeostasis and, as a result, maintain the same weight.

This is why it's important to consciously restrict the amount of energy that flows in. This is essentially the amount of food you consume. In fact, reducing energy inflow is a more effective way of creating a calorie deficit than increasing energy outflow. This is why most people who exercise but don't watch what they eat struggle to lose weight.

However, restricting the energy inflow needs to be done carefully. Because food contains both energy and nutrients, and energy inflow must be reduced without creating nutrient deficiencies. This is why we need to restrict mindfully. And it's not enough that this restriction happens every once in a while. It needs to happen across all meals and for many months if you want to see sustainable and significant weight loss.

Mindful and consistent restriction is nothing more than making smart food choices. But there are many, many methods to do it. Which method you pick matters less. What matters more is that you pick a method that suits you and your way of life and stick to it for a long time to come.

> Think about all the things that you currently eat. How much protein do you eat? What about vegetables? Carbs? Sweet foods? Chips and the like? Soft drinks? If you have to reduce 20 per cent of your total caloric intake, what would you remove or reduce and what would you not change?

#79 The science of 'calories'

Take an apple. Put it inside an insulated, oxygen-filled chamber. Seal it and place this chamber in water. Check the temperature of the water. Now, burn the apple inside the chamber completely. Check the temperature of the water again. The difference in the two temperatures will tell you how many calories that apple has.

What I described above, rather simplistically, is a bomb calorimeter, and it is how the calorie content of the various foods is calculated. One kcal is the amount of heat (energy) needed to raise the temperature of one kilogram of water by one degree Celsius. So, based on how much the water's temperature has increased, we can determine how much energy was generated by the food item inside the chamber. This is done not for all foods and dishes, but for many food items and ingredients. Then, based on the recipe, which tells us how much of each ingredient is used, the total number of calories in a dish is calculated. So, two things to keep in mind whenever you think calories:

1. *The science is accurate at the ingredient level, but not at the food or dish level.* This is because the total calories of a dish is a result of extrapolation and approximation.
2. *The total number of calories is the total amount of energy contained in the food item, but that doesn't mean your body absorbs all of it.* There is quite a bit of inefficiency in extracting energy from food, and so energy absorbed is not the same as energy consumed.

So when you see an Insta post that says one slice of pizza has 500 calories, first, remember that the number is an approximation. And, second, keep in mind that you will most probably not absorb all of it. This is why calorie counting is not an accurate means of estimating energy inflow from food. But we can work with approximations.

One kilogram of fat contains about 7,700 kcal worth of energy. This means, in order to lose 1 kilo of fat from your body, you need to create a cumulative calorie deficit of about 7,700 kcal. This need not be done in a day or in any specific period of time. Whenever you accumulate this deficit, you will lose a kilo. So, if you want to lose 10 kilos, you need to accumulate an overall deficit of 77,000 kcal. How you do this and how fast you do this is completely up to you.

For example, if you can create a deficit of exactly 500 kcal per day and do it every day, you'll lose 1 kilo of fat in 15.4 days. But this level of precision doesn't happen in real life. So, leaning on approximations and zooming out, if you can create a monthly average deficit of roughly 300–600 kcal, you will have accumulated a deficit of about 9,000–18,000 kcal, and you can expect to lose about 1–2 kilos every month.

So, skip the specifics and try not to get stuck with complicated calculations. Instead, focus on the fundamentals necessary to reduce energy inflow and increase energy outflow. The math will always add up.

> Did you know that the number of calories in an apple can vary from 50 to 120? If calorie estimation of a simple apple can vary so much, how about complex food items like kadhai paneer or dal makhani? Considering different homes and restaurants use different recipes and cook with different ingredients used at different quantities, do you think it is possible to come up with an accurate number? How practically relevant do you think any of the calorie calculations are?

#80 Weight loss using a framework

There are parallels we can draw between various parts of life. If you observe closely, a person who is great at one aspect of life might struggle with another aspect that essentially uses the same fundamental concept. For instance, you may be great at organising your house but may struggle to organise your training for the week. Or you could be a natural in understanding priorities at work but may find it impossible to do the same when it comes to lifestyle.

This is why mental models and analogies are very powerful. Once you are able to see the underlying fundamental concepts that govern these different parts of life and understand them, you can take control of the parts of life that you struggle with. That's precisely what we're going to do here. And if you are someone who likes such frameworks to help make decisions, the framework-based approach to weight loss will suit you perfectly.

In the nutrition section of this book, we discussed the practical nutrition framework in detail. In a nutshell, the idea was to find a balance between health (vegetables and fruits), strength (protein-rich foods), comfort (starchy foods), luxury (fatty foods) and fun (sweet foods). Now, since the focus is weight loss, we're simply going to apply this framework to reduce energy inflow without reducing nutrient inflow.

Here is how you do it. Three simple steps:

1. *Maximise health and strength.* Whenever you eat, make sure most of your meal is about health and strength. This means that roughly two-thirds to three-fourths of your food intake should be vegetables, fruits and protein-rich foods.
2. *Optimise comfort.* Since we're trying to restrict energy without depriving ourselves of micronutrients, limiting starch becomes necessary. Not because carbohydrates somehow make you fat, but because they contain mostly energy and very little vitamins and minerals on a per calorie basis. So, restrict starch to about a fourth (or less) of your meal on average.
3. *Minimise luxury and fun* for a while. You're on a mission, and this is not the time for a lot of luxury or fun. Your goal is to lose weight, and for that you need a certain amount of discipline. So, minimise oily, fried, fatty, creamy, rich and sugary foods. You don't have to give them up completely, but make sure they add up to only 5–10 per cent of your overall food intake.

That's it. Remember that this is a framework-based approach and hence will not involve weighing, measuring or calorie counting. The idea is to apply the framework to every meal, make simple decisions on what and how much to eat and do it consistently for the long term. Simply following these three steps will enable you to get enough protein and fibre, reduce empty calories and not overeat. This, when clubbed with enough exercise and daily activity, will create the calorie deficit necessary to lose weight.

So, don't overthink the specifics. Just understand the framework, trust the process and do the work.

> *Think about what you ate in your previous meal. How would you change the items and their proportions based on the framework explained? Can you try making similar changes to your next meal?*

#81 Weight loss using a strategy

When you're trying to lose weight, you're on a calorie budget. That's it. That's the concept. I can end this chapter right here and I'm sure you'll figure it out. The power of a strategy-based approach is that once you understand the concept, everything else starts 'making sense'. Decisions become simpler and next steps become clearer.

Think back to a time when you were living on a budget. This could have been at a different stage in your adult life. Or when you were in college. Or maybe when your parents put you on a budget to help you understand the value of money. If you're one of the lucky ones who has never experienced being on a budget, don't worry, I'll explain it below.

When you're on a budget, you don't have much money to spend. So you need to be strategic about your expenses. And strategic spending revolves around one easy-to-understand rule: *Spend on the essentials and not on the non-essentials.*

Say you have ₹30,000 to spend this month and you live in a city. What will you spend it on? Rent, electricity, fuel, internet, laundry and food? Or movies, parties, shoes and drinks? Simple question and easy answer. Now, apply the same concept to food.

Say you have 1,500 kcal to eat every day and you have to prioritise health. What will you eat? Vegetables, fruits, meat, dairy and lentils? Or fried rice, gravy, chips, milkshakes and cakes?

The essentials for health during a weight loss phase are just protein and vegetables. Everything else, to be completely honest, is not. In other words, if you eat nothing but protein and vegetables, you will get all the macronutrients you need to stay healthy. It may not be fun, you may not be happy and the effort may not be sustainable. But you will not find a concern in any of your health markers (assuming you're eating enough and a reasonable variety of foods).

So, the first step is to mentally acknowledge that you will only eat what is necessary, and brutally minimise everything that is unnecessary. Practically, this means that before you eat anything, you need to ask yourself a simple but hard question: 'Is this necessary?' If the answer is no, don't eat it. If the answer is yes, ask yourself: 'Am I hungry?' If the answer is no, don't eat it. If the answer is yes, eat a little, and repeat the process.

Why? Because you are on a calorie budget, and you don't have the privilege of spending (eating) without thinking. Will this be hard? Of course. Living on a budget is meant to be hard. Won't it be too hard to sustain? Probably. And that's why we need some layers.

Living on a budget for a few weeks is not too challenging. You can be brutal about your choices, expect high levels of discipline and deprive yourself of all things fun and fancy. But, if you have to live on a budget for months or years, you need to be *more* strategic. And that means learning to deal with the grey areas. Here is how you do it.

Spend 80–90 per cent of your budget on the essentials and only 10–20 per cent on non-essentials. That means, ₹24,000–27,000 per month for rent, electricity, fuel, internet, laundry and food and ₹3,000–6,000 per month for movies, parties, shoes and drinks. Or 1,200–1,350 kcal per day for vegetables, fruits, meat, dairy and lentils and 150–300 kcal per day for fried rice, gravy, chips, milkshakes and cakes. Still not easy, but definitely more sustainable.

But here's the best part about the strategy-based approach—you can do this your way. It's your strategy. The stricter you are, the faster the results but the shorter the sustainability window. And the more lax you are, the slower the results but the longer the sustainability window. What do you prefer? Hard and fast or slow and sustainable?

Figure it out, strategise, get to work.

> What would your strategic approach look like? Can you group your usual foods into essential and non-essential? How would you like to split up the percentages?
>
> While you think about percentages and how hard you are willing to work, what do you think about modulating intensity? A few weeks of really hard work with only 5 per cent from non-essentials followed by a relatively easy week with about 20 per cent from non-essentials and so on. Do you think you can build a cool strategy for yourself using this approach?

#82 Weight loss using rules

Throughout the city, there are these little implements that keep us safe. Literally hundreds of these can be found in every city, and they save millions of lives worldwide daily. They don't move, they are not high on tech and they don't even use text. Their only job is to tell us when it's safe to drive and when it's not. The humble traffic light is an excellent example of the rule-based approach.

When you approach a traffic light, you have one simple set of rules to follow. If you see red, stop. If you see orange, proceed with caution. And, if you see green, move forward. This applies irrespective of what time of the day it is, or whether or not there are other vehicles on the road. If everyone can diligently follow this one set of rules, we can ensure everyone's safety at that intersection. Rules can be that powerful, and this applies to weight loss too.

So, here are five nutrition rules that will help you lose weight in a healthy and sustainable manner:

1. *Eat during meal times and only during meal times.* Eat two or three good meals a day but nothing in between. No snacking, no grazing and no saying yes simply because someone offered you something to eat. If it is not the time to eat, don't eat.
2. *Eat lean protein and vegetables in every meal.* Every meal should contain some form of lean protein and some vegetable matter. If necessary, some starch. The protein can be anything that is not

fatty, oily or fried. Meat, seafood, low-fat paneer, tofu, tempeh or protein supplements are great options. The vegetable can be any vegetable, except potatoes and corn, because corn is a grain and potatoes contain mostly starch. If nothing is available, even onions and tomatoes will do. If that is also not available, a fruit can be a substitute. The starch can be dosa, roti, idli, rice, millets, pasta or whatever you like, but it should not be fatty, oily or fried and its quantity should be as low as possible.
3. *Minimise sweet and fatty foods.* Anything that is sweet, oily, fried, rich or creamy should be minimised. What is minimal is a call you can take based on your current food habits. Don't get lost in the specifics. It's a rule. Interpret it in the best and most effective way possible. Don't try to find loopholes.
4. *Eat as slowly as possible.* We've already discussed why it's important to not wolf down your food and what happens if you do. So, chew every bite thoroughly, pause between bites and slow down. Aim to spend at least 15 minutes finishing your plate of food. After all, you are only going to eat two or three times a day. Take your time and savour every bite.
5. *Don't overeat.* We've learnt about satiety. Now it's time to apply that knowledge and skill in real life. Whatever you eat, eat below satiety. This is definitely the most important rule when it comes to weight loss. Because this one rule can ensure that you eat less and enable that calorie deficit to be created.

Unlike the framework-based approach or the strategy-based approach, the rule-based approach involves little to no thinking—simply follow the rules. It's perfect for people who don't want to invest any mental energy in thinking about the issue and, instead, simply prefer to act. Also, for many of us, there are times when we are busy or focused on other parts of life that we may prefer to simply follow rules instead of strategising and using up mental bandwidth. If this is you, these five rules are all you need. You're ready to start from your very next meal.

> How are you with following rules? Do you prefer thinking and strategising or do you prefer a following a set of rules?
>
> Irrespective of what method you prefer, you can use different methods at different times. At what stages of your life will a rule-based approach simplify things for you? Travel? Times of high work stress? Festival season?

#83 Weight loss using diets

Diets have been around for decades. There are hundreds, if not thousands, of diets are available today: low fat, low carb, keto, paleo, zone, mediterranean, Atkins, raw food, weight watchers and so many more. The problem with so much choice is that it becomes virtually impossible to understand which diet is the best one. Allow me to simplify it for you—all diets are the same.

Because all weight loss diets are essentially a set of restrictions that are meant to help reduce energy inflow.

If you view weight loss diets with the fundamental understanding of nutrition concepts we've learnt till now, it will be clear that all diets are just sets of restrictions, each one unique. But the end goal is the same—use these restrictions to reduce the energy inflow. Why? Because it all finally comes down to thermodynamics, and a calorie deficit is required for weight loss.

The low-fat diet restricts energy by restricting the amount of fat you can eat. The keto diet does the same thing by severely restricting the amount of carbohydrates you can eat. The paleo diet does this by restricting sugars, grains, lentils and legumes. The plant-based diet does this by restricting all animal products. And intermittent fasting does it by restricting the duration of eating in a day. But, in essence, they are all simply different sets of restrictions.

Do keep in mind that there may be other benefits to each of these diets. But if your goal is weight loss, then any of them will work. But there are two major drawbacks to this approach.

First, most, if not all, diets will successfully reduce the amount of food you eat and hence reduce the number of calories you consume (and absorb). But they work only in the short term. This is because most are too restrictive. And when you feel this, in spite of your best intentions, you are able to sustain your efforts for only a few weeks or, at most, a few months.

The second drawback is that when you're on a diet, you are told exactly what to eat, when to eat and how much to eat. You don't really learn much about the why behind it all. And so, once you're done with the diet, you simply go back to eating the way you used to. Because one, this new way of eating is too restrictive and, two, you don't know enough to modify this new way to make it sustainable. And slowly, but surely, the lost weight starts coming back.

So if you're someone who enjoys diets, go for it. But be informed that it is mostly a short-term solution. And here is how you can use it smartly—once you're done with the diet, switch to one of the three long-term approaches I've outlined earlier (exercise, strength train, walk) and continue the journey. This way you get to attack the problem using different intensities and different strategies, thereby helping yourself stay consistent in the long term.

> What do you think about diets? Have you tried them? Were you successful? Did you like the experience? Did you find it sustainable or too hard? Instead of viewing diets as solutions, could you view them as tools for short-term weight loss? And how about a hybrid approach using diets, strategies and frameworks?

#84 Not maximal. Not minimal. Optimal

Too hard, and you'll break it. Too soft, and you won't make a dent. Just right, and you have yourself a beautiful pot. Pottery is a wonderful art form and it doesn't have much in common with weight loss. But what we can learn from it is the importance of optimality.

There is a rate at which you can lose weight without affecting your health or pushing your body into survival mode. This is the optimal rate of weight loss. While it varies from person to person, if you can figure out what this is for you, you can lose weight with less resistance from your body and do it for much longer.

The optimal rate of weight loss is anywhere between 0.25 and 1.5 per cent of your body weight every week. This is a big range, and it is so for a reason. But, let's remember the relationship between intensity and duration—they are indirectly proportional. That means, in weight loss terms, the higher your rate of weight loss, the shorter you can keep that up for and vice versa.

At the start of your weight loss journey, you will lose a lot of weight quickly. It's not uncommon to see people lose 1–3 per cent of their body weight every week. This is because a lot of weight lost is due to water being lost. When we eat without restrictions, we are in a bloated state because we tend to consume a lot of starches and sugars, which cause water retention. So, when we start restricting energy inflow, we invariably restrict starches and sugars and hence retain less water. But this high rate of initial weight loss is not sustainable because we simply can't lose fat at the same rate as water.

A couple of weeks in, once water retention is reduced, your rate of weight loss will drop to about 0.5–1.5 per cent of your body weight per week, depending on how big a calorie deficit you're creating. And then in a few more weeks, it will drop even more. And that's OK.

As long as you're continuing to lose weight and losing at least 0.25 per cent of your body weight every week, you are still well on track. Some weeks will be better than this and some weeks will see no change on the scale, but keep in mind that there are many variables here. As long as your body weight is following a downward trend, you're good. Keep going without worrying about how quickly it's happening. If, and only if, you stop losing weight for two continuous weeks or more, take another look at your energy inflow and outflow and make changes as needed.

The optimal rate of weight loss is the rate at which you can lose weight without feeling deprived and without pushing your body too hard. Figuring this out is not easy. But, if you want to make a beautiful pot, you need to learn to apply just the right amount of pressure and at the right times. And the only way to do that is experimentation and patience.

> In your previous efforts to lose weight, how did you perceive your results? Were you expecting to lose 1 kilo or more every week? When that didn't happen, how did it make you feel? Now that you understand why optimal is important and what the optimal rate of weight loss is, do you think you will approach your weight loss journey with more patience?

#85 Save what you need, burn what you don't

When we lose weight, we ideally want to trim only the fat and retain everything else as is. But pure fat loss rarely happens. Because when we lose weight, we lose different things from our bodies. Typically, this includes water, fat, muscle and bone. Everyone's weight loss journey involves losing all these things, and only the amounts vary. The difference between random weight loss and healthy weight loss is the ratio of how much each of these is lost.

While fat loss is a part of any weight loss, the question is how big a part it is. The goal is to make it the largest part of the weight that is lost. We need to maximise the amount of fat lost and minimise the amount of muscle lost. To do that, we need to keep an eye on three things:

1. *Muscle stimulation*. The single most effective way to prevent muscle and bone loss is strength or resistance training. Because, when it comes to breaking down muscle tissue to create energy, your body tends to choose the ones that are not regularly used. When you strength train regularly, the muscles of your body are stimulated regularly and hence spared by the body. So, do some form of resistance exercise that makes your muscles work, especially when trying to lose weight. This will enable you to minimise the amount of muscle and bone lost and make your weight loss mostly fat loss.

2. *Rate of weight loss.* How quickly you lose weight is determined by how big a calorie deficit you create. And the quantum of the deficit determines where the energy to fill the deficit comes from. If the deficit is extremely low, your body may not find the need to touch your fat stores, and hence there may be little to no fat loss. But if the deficit is too big, your body will not be able to address it quickly through fat alone, because mobilising and burning fat is a slow process. And so it will pull energy by also breaking down muscle tissue, leading to loss in muscle mass. So, try not to get greedy for too much too soon. Instead, focus on sustainability by losing weight in the optimal weight loss range.
3. *Stress and sleep.* Working out is only one half of the effort. The other half, and the more important half in my opinion, is recovery. Because when you exercise, you are applying stress and forcing the body to somehow cope. But it is when you rest that you allow the body to adapt to the stress, recover and become better. For the body to adapt and recover, it needs optimal amounts of sleep and stress. Insufficient sleep or too much stress could force the body into survival mode. This could cause hormonal dysregulation, especially high cortisol levels, which could cause fat accumulation and increased muscle loss.

So, while pure fat loss is a very rare phenomenon, working on retaining as much muscle as possible while losing fat is key to ensuring you end up lean and strong, and not skinny and weak.

> If I said you could lose 10 kilos in three weeks, but more than half of it would be muscle loss, would you go for it? Or would you prefer losing the same 10 kilos in fifteen to twenty weeks but ensuring 90 per cent of it is fat loss?

#86 Embrace hunger

Hunger is an uncomfortable feeling, and it's designed to be so for everyone. While for some hunger is still very much a part of life every day, for many of us today, it is an unfamiliar feeling. Living in an age of abundance, we rarely find ourselves hungry for more than a couple of hours. We are surrounded by food and spoilt for choice, and we certainly use the situation to its best.

While we need to acknowledge and empathise with the population that faces chronic hunger, if food abundance is your reality, it's possible that your relationship with hunger is stressful. You probably have a low tolerance for hunger and treat it as an emergency. This is understandable, because a lot of what you do when you're hungry is driven more by hormones and less by logic and common sense. But when it comes to weight loss, tolerating hunger is necessary.

You already know that you need to create a calorie deficit to lose weight. For that, you have to provide your body with less energy than it needs. But here is something about the body that you need to always remember—your body will not burn stored energy (fat) when you provide it with new energy from the outside (food).

Let's assume that you have created a calorie deficit by ensuring that the energy outflow was higher than the energy inflow. That means the body isn't getting all the energy it needs. So, at multiple points of time during the day, your stomach will inevitably be empty and your body will need energy. When this happens, you will feel hunger. At this point, if you treat it as an emergency and immediately eat to address that feeling, your body will use this new energy to satisfy its needs instead of pulling fat out of cells and burning it to create the energy needed. In plain words, you are not giving your body a chance to use the stored energy. And that means you are not giving your body a chance to burn fat.

So hunger, in a way, is a good thing when you're trying to lose weight. But like all good things, there is a sweet spot. Addressing hunger immediately doesn't help, but letting it progress to extreme levels doesn't help either. Because when hunger gets to a certain point, it becomes an actual emergency for the body, and the brain treats it like one. It releases hormones that make you focus overly on food. All you think about is food. You are aggressive and in a hurry (to find food). Your sensitivity to the taste and smell of food is heightened, and you're disinterested in pretty much everything else. This is a survival tactic and meant to ensure you don't accidentally starve yourself to death.

So, if you continue to deprive yourself of food beyond this point, other systems get hit. You start feeling dizzy, get headaches, develop acidity and so on. Once you get to this 'extreme hunger' zone, your behaviour is not fully under your control. There is a very good chance that you eat foods that contain quick energy, which are typically foods that are rich in sugar, starch and fat and not useful from a weight loss perspective. You also tend to eat fast and hence eat more food than you really need.

Clearly, hunger is something you need to embrace and use to your advantage smartly in your weight loss journey. But the real trick is to learn to tolerate mild to moderate hunger without letting yourself get extremely hungry.

> How do you behave when you're hungry? Do you treat it as an emergency or are you calm and composed? How about when you are extremely hungry? Do you see how your control of your choices is compromised during such times and how that drives you to eat more than you need to?

#87 Why do some people lose weight faster than others?

If you took two people of the same weight and had them do the same training programme and eat the same food, the chances of the two of them losing the same amount of weight is extremely low. Depending on who these two people are, the difference in results could range from very little to crazy. Why does this happen? If it's not something obvious like extra walking or secretly exercising more, the usual answer is genetics. But what does that really mean? I bet if you asked this question, most times there would either be silence or a response that doesn't make sense when you think about it a second time.

The answer is actually quite easy to understand—efficiency. Let me explain.

Physically, we are all essentially (organic) machines that procure energy and convert it into other forms of energy or create matter out of it. The process of procuring energy is not simple. We need to get our energy from other animals and plants by eating them. But when we eat them, they are not in energy form. We need to break them down and extract the energy (and nutrients) from them. This is a process that starts in the mouth and ends in the small intestine, where the water and digested nutrients are absorbed into the bloodstream. What was not absorbed is pushed to the large intestine and then excreted.

Similarly, the process of expending energy is not simple either. Nutrients and energy are stored in our body in three forms: glucose in the blood ready to be used, glucose in the form of glycogen (a complex form of sugar) stored in the muscles and liver, and fat in fat cells. When we need to expend energy to do anything (be it lifting a weight or batting an eyelid), we need to expend energy. While we can use glucose and glycogen for immediate needs, the long-term supply of energy has to come from fat. And converting fat to energy is actually a two-step process. First, the fat needs to be pulled out of fat cells (fat mobilisation), and then it needs to be broken down and oxidised to be converted into usable energy (fat oxidation or burning).

I don't know exactly how efficient these processes are. But I can guarantee you that they are not 100 per cent efficient, and they are definitely not at the same level of efficiency for two different people. Person A might have a high efficiency in the energy expenditure process and hence burn calories from fat very easily. As a result, they can create a calorie deficit easily and lose weight faster. Person B might have a low efficiency and so, even though they are putting in the work, the rate at which they can expend energy is low and that limits them from doing more and creating the necessary calorie deficit. So, Person B is not losing weight fast enough. And this is not because Person B is not putting in their best effort, but because, genetically, their energy expending efficiency is low.

On the other hand, there could be differences in energy procurement efficiency too. Person C may eat a lot of calories but not absorb much of them, but Person D might eat less overall food but absorb more. This will obviously mean that the net energy inflow is higher in Person D than in Person C, and that will affect their ability to create the required calorie deficit even though they may be expending the same amount of energy or more as Person C.

So the next time you think about comparing your progress with someone else's, remember that it's not a fair comparison. Everyone loses weight at different rates based on multiple variables. The best you can do is to focus on the variables that are under your control. Do that, and don't sweat the rest.

> Have you ever felt like you lose weight slower or faster than others? How did this make you feel? Now that you understand that each of us have different levels of efficiency in absorbing and expending energy, can you view weight loss not as a competition but as consistent betterment?

#88 Pills, potions and procedures

Everything we have discussed until now is about effort. In other words, we've learnt about what you can do in order to lose weight and improve your health. But, for some of us, effort is not the only concern. In other words, even if we do everything right, the scale doesn't do what it's supposed to do. Let's understand this better.

First, let's be clear that nothing can change the laws of thermodynamics. Nothing. That means that no matter who you are and what your health and genetic make-up are like, the fundamental requirement for weight loss remains the same—energy outflow has to be higher than energy inflow.

But, based on what we learnt about efficiency, what some conditions can do is make it harder or almost impossible to increase energy outflow or decrease energy inflow. This can impair weight loss significantly. There are conditions that affect fat mobilisation (moving fat out of fat cells) and hence make it harder to burn calories. There are also conditions that cause hormonal dysregulation, which results in an unpredictable and high appetite, which makes it very hard to reduce energy inflow. And there are even conditions that cause BMR to be extremely low, which also severely hampers energy outflow. What this tells us is that the same effort from different people will not produce the same results.

On one end of the spectrum, there are people who train hard a few days a week, eat fairly well and end up losing fat, building muscle and getting in top shape. On the other end of the spectrum, there are people who train every day, watch every morsel of what they eat, walk many kilometres and take a variety of supplements only to see average results. While only a small percentage of people are at these ends of the spectrum, there are quite a few of us who are close to these ends.

If you find that you are closer to the sucky end of this spectrum and are struggling to lose weight in spite of your best efforts, here are two tips for you:

1. *Don't compare your results with that of others.* Work with what you have. Because it really doesn't matter how quickly someone else is progressing or how easy it is for them. You are only trying to be better than your previous self. Focus on you, your efforts and your progress. Do more or less based on the rate of your progress without letting someone else's journey affect you.
2. *If you are doing everything you can and are still finding it impossible to make reasonable progress, consider weight loss procedures or pills.* Which procedure, what pill, how often, how much and for how long will entirely depend on the specifics of your situation. So be sure to talk to a doctor, discuss your condition in detail and work together in charting out a plan for yourself. This plan should contain a combination of lifestyle changes and medical intervention based on your current situation and future goals.

Whatever route you take, always remember one thing—there is no need and no place for shame or judgement. Your weight loss journey is precisely that—*your journey*. No one should feel the need to judge or comment on it. The goal is to take control of your body weight, manage it well in the long term and ensure you are fit and healthy for yourself and your loved ones. The way I see it, you should only be kind to and proud of yourself for doing this, regardless of how you're doing it.

> Have you considered using pills or procedures to help with weight loss? Did you consider this after putting in a lot of effort to change your lifestyle? Did you, at any point, feel guilt or shame about this consideration? And did this chapter help you feel differently about it?

#89 Weight loss in ten simple actions

Now that we have discussed the details of how weight loss works and the different ways to make it happen, let's simplify and summarise it.

1. *Exercise four to five days a week*, which includes two to three days of strength work. These five days can be a combination of different types of exercise (the four Ss) but ensure the total calorie expenditure is at least 2,000 per week. This will enable you to increase energy outflow temporarily and also build muscle, which will increase your BMR and help you increase energy outflow in the long term.
2. *Walk as much as you can every day.* From a health perspective, 10,000 steps isn't special. But from a weight loss perspective, you want to increase calorie burn. And since you burn 25–50 calories for every 1,000 steps, depending on your body weight, body composition and walking speed, try and get close to that number. Because 10,000 steps will mean you burn 250–500 calories each day from walking. If you can do more, go for it. If you can't do 10,000, start where you are now and increase your total step count by 1,000 per day every week.
3. *Get 1.25–1.75 grams of protein per kilo of your body weight every day and eat protein in every meal.* This serves two purposes. First, protein is very satiating. Eating protein in every meal will help you feel fuller sooner and stay fuller for longer, thereby preventing you from overeating unintentionally during another meal or between

meals. And second, getting enough protein (along with strength training) will ensure your body loses mostly fat and doesn't eat up muscle.
4. *Eat vegetables in every meal* and target getting in three to five servings of vegetables and fruits every day. In addition to nourishing you with micronutrients, vegetables and fruits are low in calorie density and will fill you up, thereby preventing you from overeating.
5. *Eat starch as a side.* Meals that are dominated by starch tend to be high in calories and low in nutrients, which is precisely what we don't want. So, eat starch, but don't let it dominate the meal. Simply keep the quantity on the lower side. Think back to the practical nutrition framework—comfort (starchy foods) is important for sustainability, but too much comfort will be counterproductive.
6. *Keep sweet and fatty foods well under control.* You don't have to give up sugar, fat or anything for that matter. Because giving things up only leads to feelings of deprivation in a few weeks. So eat them, but be very cautious about how often and how much you're eating. Think back to the practical nutrition framework—fun (sweet foods) and luxury (fatty foods) are important, but when you're on a calorie budget, you need to keep these to a minimum.
7. *Don't graze or eat unnecessarily.* That means, eat during meal times and only during meal times. You can eat as many meals as is right for you, but plan ahead and eat only during those times. Don't eat without reason, don't graze or nibble on things when you're around food and say no to food if it is offered when you don't need it.
8. *Don't overeat.* Irrespective of what you eat, stop eating before you are fully satisfied. Because weight loss finally comes down to creating that optimal calorie deficit, and overeating and

eating unnecessarily are the quickest ways to make that deficit disappear.
9. *Sleep at least fifty hours every week.* Different splits and patterns will suit different people. Figure out what works best for you and get it done. Because you will not be able to do what is explained in steps 1 to 8 if you don't sleep enough.
10. *Manage stress.* What stressors you face are unique to you, but the consequence of unmanaged stress on weight loss is the same for everyone—inability to sustain effort and stay consistent. And without consistency, there are exactly zero chances of progress. While you can't prevent stress from showing up in your life, learning to be aware of stress, improving your stress tolerance and managing your stress effectively will make this whole thing a lot easier.

The first two actions are meant to help increase energy outflow, the next six to help decrease energy inflow and the last two are enablers that make it possible to consistently do the first eight actions. Simple. Not easy. But, if you are serious about losing weight and improving your health, all of this is definitely doable.

> At this point you have all the tools, knowledge and skills necessary to lose weight. Do you think you can take control of your weight loss or weight management journey? Which of these ten simple actions are you already doing well? And which are the ones you need to work on?

SECTION 7

CONSISTENCY

#90   It all adds up

You receive a phone call. It's from a food delivery person, and she says your friend has sent you a package. You're happy. You wait for her at the door, curious to know what has been sent for you. You receive it and immediately take a peek. It's a cake! Decadent, rich and scarily delicious looking cake. It's got all the bits you love. And you're certain it's going to be soft and moist with just enough crunch from the toppings. You're excited.

But it is only when you take the cake out of the bag that you realise how large it is. When you call your friend to thank them, you realise it's a 1.5-kilo cake. Your friend ordered it because they knew you'd love it, but a smaller size was unavailable. So, you now have a delicious but huge cake sitting in your fridge. You know you can't eat it all. It's not possible, you say. Regardless of how delicious it is, how can one person eat such a massive cake, you exclaim. *I should cut it into small portions and distribute it among our friends*, you think. So, you take another spoonful and stash it back in the fridge so you can share it tomorrow.

The next day, you get busy with work. You don't get a chance to actually cut the cake into smaller portions, make packages and send it to your friends. So, you eat a little more, but most of the cake is still there, staring at you every time you open the fridge. A couple more days go by, and now it isn't fresh anymore for you to send it to your friends. So, this scary-looking, delicious thing lives in your fridge. And in the next ten days or so, little by little, a couple of small spoons at a time, very gradually you peck on it. You eat only a small amount at a time. You never eat till you feel full or disgusted. Sometimes you eat it because you're really feeling like eating cake. And sometimes you eat just because it's there. But eventually, one day, you open the fridge and that mountain of a cake that was staring at you is now just a tiny piece. It dawns on you that you have actually eaten the whole 1.5-kilo cake all by yourself. You've done the impossible.

This is consistency.

The ability and patience to do a little bit regularly for a long period of time is the basis of consistency, and it applies to everything in fitness. Not just exercise, but everything. How consistently do you eat enough protein? How consistently do you overeat? How consistently do you sleep enough? How consistently do you make smart food choices? These are all questions that are very relevant to your progress, because consistency is another double-edged sword that you need to learn to wield to your advantage.

We always overestimate what we can achieve in two weeks but underestimate what we can achieve in two years. And that's why it doesn't matter how great your programme, coach, equipment and gym are if you are not consistent. Because consistency is the Holy Grail. It's the magic pill you've been looking for. It's the shortcut that will get you to your goals in record time. *Consistency is, without a shred of doubt, the skill you need to master.*

> What are three things you do very consistently in your life? Going to work? Showering (I hope!)? Reading? Sharing reels? Being on time? Whatever they are, what helps you be consistent with these? The fun factor? Have you built habits over years? Discipline? What can you learn from these parts of your life that you can apply to exercise, nutrition and sleep?

#91 Betterment is the goal

Most of us want to look and move like Olympic athletes. It's hard not to want that. They look great and move beautifully. And they perform feats so incredible that they demand admiration. But they live very different lives. What we see when they perform is the beautiful tip of the iceberg, which sits on top of layers and layers of solid ice formed over years. What we don't see is everything else. The years of discipline and relentless practice. The sacrifices, pain and laser focus. The infallible intent to win. The will to put themselves through extreme discomfort. And the ability to recover and do this over and over again.

What we know but don't always remember is that we're not going to live that life. We don't have to. We're not gunning for the Olympics or for the silver screen here. What we're here for is to look, feel and function better. To be better versions of ourselves.

So there is no competition to worry about. No timeline to get to your goals. And definitely no prize or national pride to strive for. Because the race is only against our previous selves and we are our only competition.

This is an important realisation. Because, in today's world of rapid communication, oversharing and digital editing, it's very easy to get overwhelmed and misguided on how much and how quickly someone else is supposedly achieving something.

A forty-year-old accountant from Gurgaon who goes to the gym a few days a week and plays badminton every weekend compares herself to a professional athlete from Norway and feels like she should work a lot harder. A recreational dancer who has recently lost quite a few kilos and found his love for dancing watches a few reels of some super athletic kids doing unimaginable dance steps and feels there is no point in trying to get better anymore because he can never be as good as them. There are millions of such wonderful people, putting in as much effort as they can in spite of their busy lives and nonathletic pasts, who still feel demotivated and insufficient when they compare themselves to others.

The truth is that the majority of us are not going to compete. And definitely not with the people we see on social media. The fact remains that we are just trying to improve the quality of our very own lives. We just want to be better.

And that means you don't have to compare. You don't have to rush. And you don't have to stress. It also means you don't have to be perfect or try to be the best. What you need to do is to strive to be slightly better than you were yesterday. And if you are able to do that consistently day after day, you can be assured that the future you will be better than the past you.

So, strive. Not to be the best, but to be better. Try. Not to be perfect, but to progress. Because better is what everyone wants. Even the best.

> How do you want to be better this year? Can you be specific about it? Do you want to look a certain way or feel better or perform more? What are some simple metrics that you can measure that will help you understand if you are making progress?

#92 Are you uncomfortable enough?

How are you? This is one of the most commonly asked questions in the world. And the most common answer to this question is some form of good, OK or fine. And that's a problem. Let me explain.

Humans are adaptable creatures. We had to adapt in order to survive and evolve. And thanks to this natural ability to tolerate things, even today we can live in different conditions (physically and emotionally) at varying levels of comfort. And discomfort. Typically, at the initial stages of discomfort, we're not happy. We fight it. We try to change it. But, soon, we get used to it. We learn to live and laugh, in spite of the discomfort.

This is especially true with health and fitness. Most of us today have some form of struggle around health or fitness. It could be a disease, or a condition or maybe just an ache, pain or niggle. Almost everyone has something that we are not happy about. But, as nature intended, we tolerate it. And we don't find the need or the drive to fix it. At least, not right away. And so, every day billions of people tolerate thousands of different types of physical and mental discomforts and still live good, OK or fine lives.

Make no mistake—most, if not all, of us want 'better' in our lives. We would surely like fewer pills and problems, less pain and more energy, strength and happiness. But, to go from where we are now to that 'better' place, we need to make some fairly significant changes.

More often than not, these changes are around lifestyle. Specifically, around how well we eat, sleep, move and manage stress. And that's where we are stuck—in a zone where we realise we want better and know we need to change but are still unable to find it in us to actually change.

Why does this happen? Because though we are living in discomfort, we are still largely satisfied with how things are.

The obese twenty-year-old does not love carrying that extra weight. But he is still having a good life in college with friends, food and fun. The forty-five-year-old dance teacher with chronic knee pain is not enjoying the pain that shoots up every time she has to demo a step. But she is still living a happy life respected by her students, doing what she loves and learning every day. The hardworking and sleep-deprived cardiac surgeon with recurring ulcers is not unaware that this is not a healthy lifestyle. But he is living an inspired life that is fuelled by the drive to succeed and the passion to save others.

What does it take for these people, and the rest of us, to go from tolerating discomfort to acting on it? Enough discomfort.

Because we will take the first steps towards change only when we are unhappy enough with our current situation. And so we're left with two choices. Wait for the injuries, diseases and pains to intensify naturally and reach a point where they are intolerable. Or proactively address the parts we are unhappy with. If we pick the former, we are choosing to be controlled by pain and discomfort. But if we pick the latter, we are choosing to be in control.

> Are you uncomfortable enough today? In the areas that you want to improve, be it weight loss or strength or speed or health, do you feel a strong dissatisfaction that could push you to take the first steps necessary for change?

#93 Motivation wanes but habits compound

No one enjoys exercise. I'm sure you've heard a lot of people say 'I love to exercise', but physiologically, this is not possible. Exercise, by definition, involves doing work that uses up energy and muscle power and stresses the body's various components enough for them to need recovery. In such a scenario, stress hormones are released, and no one is really enjoying it like they do when having pleasure. Going for a run might be fun, but it's not fun like eating a slice of cake or laughing with your loved ones.

So, then, why do people do it? How do they do it consistently? And how can you make it a fun and sustainable part of your life? The answer is complicated from a psychological and physiological perspective, but very simple from a logical perspective.

Dissatisfaction. That's where it starts. To take the first steps towards a change, you need to be dissatisfied enough with your current state of being. We discussed this in detail in the previous chapter. Assuming this is the case and that you have started, what next? How do you move past the first steps?

Motivation. You need a reason to do whatever it is you have to do. In the case of exercise, you need a reason to put yourself through physical discomfort. Your reason may be anything. Aesthetic change, improved functionality, doctor's orders—anything. This reason will give you enough of a push to build on your first steps and move forward.

In a practical scenario, dissatisfaction will get you to sign up at a gym and motivation will push you to go to the gym for the first few days or weeks. But this exact scenario happens to literally millions of people at the start of every year. What next? How do you stay consistent after the first few weeks?

Discipline. The practice of doing the things you need to do even when you don't want to do them. It's not easy and it's not fun. But discipline is an important part of long-term fitness. Because it will train you to do the right things even when you don't feel like it. And that's important, because given how abundant food is and how sedentary we are, very rarely will you naturally feel like doing all the right things. But another reason that we need to embrace and practise discipline is that it paves the way for the next and most important step towards long-term fitness.

Habits. If you can get to a stage where you are able to do something without having to reason with yourself about whether you should do it or not, you have successfully built a habit. Habits are important. But doubly so when it comes to things we don't naturally enjoy. Exercise, eating vegetables in every meal, turning off screens and going to bed early are all examples. The people who exercise consistently and have been doing so for years don't do it because they are always motivated. Or because they somehow enjoy being in physical discomfort. They do it because they have successfully built a habit of exercising. In fact, their habit is so strong that they are happy to move around other aspects of their life to accommodate exercise. This is what people mean when they say 'you need to make it happen'. Easily done by those who have the habit, but mostly impossible for those who don't.

The key takeaway here is that consistency is heavily dependent on habits, and habits can be built by anyone. And that means you don't have to be special or work extra hard to get fit—you simply need to build the right habits.

Because dissatisfaction can get you started and motivation can push you forward. But only habits can keep you going.

> Do you rely on motivation or on habits? How do you feel when you're high on motivation? And how does it feel when you are not motivated? Have you built habits that keep you going even when motivation drops? And what do you think about using both tools and getting the best of both worlds?

#94 Consistency is a life skill

The interesting thing about consistency is that we are both consistent and inconsistent at the same time. Everyone is consistent in some aspects of their life. And everyone struggles with consistency in some other aspects. You may not be consistent with your exercise, but you may be extremely consistent in keeping your house clean, reviewing your accounts or planning regular vacations. Someone else may be very consistent with their exercise but might struggle to consistently take breaks when needed, keep their living space clean or visit their parents.

It's entirely possible to learn about consistency from ourselves. We can look at the part of us that is consistent, understand how we are being consistent and apply those learnings to the part that is not. But this requires a lot of self-awareness, self-analysis and experimentation. If that's the way you like to do things, go for it. I can assure you that it's an interesting, involved and rewarding process.

But for most people, this is too much work. A few simple steps and a framework would work much better. If this is you, then here is what you need to do.

1. *Understand compounding.* Consistency is extremely useful, simply because it enables compounding. The 'snowball effect'. Imagine a small snowball rolling down the hill covered with snow. With every roll, it collects more snow. And it becomes bigger and

heavier. This results in its momentum increasing, which increases its speed. And this increase in speed and mass causes it to collect even more snow, which will further increase its mass and speed and so on. And at some point, it will get to a size where it is hard to believe that this massive ball of snow actually started as a tiny little thing. This is what consistency can do for you—it can help small actions accumulate in time to produce massive and almost unbelievable results.
2. *Build the right habits.* A good lifestyle is about making the right choices. Habits make it easier to do that. For example, brushing your teeth every morning and night is important for dental health and hygiene. Until it becomes a habit, it is still a choice, and you have to remember to do it every day. But once it becomes a habit, you will be able to do it without much conscious thought or deliberation about whether you should do it or not. It just happens like clockwork. In fact, it feels off when you don't do it. That's the power of a habit, and it's something you certainly need if you want to be consistent with anything.
3. *Trust the process.* The primary cause of inconsistency is a mismatch of expectations. You expect to see results quickly. When you don't see them, you lose heart and reduce or change the effort, resulting in inconsistency, which will ensure you don't see results. But if you can trust the process and remember that if you put in the right work, it's simply a matter of time before you're able to see the real effects of consistency and compounding, that results are inevitable.
4. *Be patient.* The amazing and annoying part about creating big results in the long term is that the effort is low but the progress is slow. You're not going to see much change in the first few days or weeks. But if you can be patient, trust the process and keep putting in the work, things will start looking up.

> Are you patient with yourself? It's a simple question but a loaded one. In your fitness journey, or generally in life, do you practise patience or are you in a hurry to see results? Do you agree that taking a step back, trusting the process and working without expectations will help with progress? If yes, do you think this is something you can do?

#95 Mastering consistency

Have you ever wondered why kids start school at kindergarten and very slowly make their way to twelfth grade? Why not start somewhere in the middle? Why not move faster? The obvious answer is that the syllabus will be too advanced and they won't be able to handle it. They have to learn the alphabet and integers first before moving on to grammar and algebra. Yes, but school is not just about the syllabus. It is about habits too.

When a child starts going to school, her life changes. Her day is now different. There are new demands and expectations. She needs to sleep and wake up at a certain time, spend a significant part of her day with new people in a new place, learn to do things by herself and so on. This is not easy to adapt to, and so there is a period during which she's getting used to it all. This is why classes for little kids start late and finish early. This gradually changes as they grow. Also, the focus for the first few years is simply on showing up, not running away from class and not crying for parents. Not on how much knowledge they gain. In fact, the syllabus doesn't even apply for the first couple of years. Only after these fundamentals are established are they even expected to learn, perform and have their learning tested.

While most of us understand this well, we don't understand that this applies to anyone who is struggling to be consistent with exercise too.

Once they decide to make a change, most people join a gym or sign up for a programme. And almost immediately, they are expected (by themselves) to dedicate multiple hours a week for exercise, perform movements that they never knew existed and be aware of reps, sets, steps and other metrics. It's no wonder that so many of us who start exercising with the best of intentions end up being inconsistent and give up. Because we skipped kindergarten. Because, instead of building a strong foundation like the little ones do, we jumped directly to a level that we can't handle.

And this is why the three Ds mindset for consistency works like magic, slow magic.

Do.

Do this.

Do this like that.

If you are someone who is new to exercise or struggling to stay consistent, here are three phases that will teach you the art of consistency and build a habit that will last you a long time.

Phase 1: Do. The goal of this phase is to simply 'do'. What, where, how much or how well don't matter. For the next seven to fourteen days, every day, simply do something active. It can be anything. Walking, swimming, dancing, lifting, sports or whatever else is accessible to you. There are only two requirements. One, you keep it simple. And, two, do it at the same time every day as far as possible. For example, for the next seven days, spend time in the morning doing something active. Once again, it doesn't matter what you do, how hard you work or how long you do it for. This phase is simply about building a habit of showing up. So the only goal is to show up.

Phase 2: Do this. In this second phase, we add in a layer of specificity. But we'll still keep it fairly simple. So, specify what you will do on each day but you still don't worry about how long, how hard, etc. For example, for the seven to fourteen days following phase 1, plan your week—go for a walk or jog on Monday and Tuesday, strength train on Wednesday, yoga on Thursday and so on. You simply need to define what you're going to do and do it. Your goal in this phase is to show up and do what you said you'd do.

Phase 3: Do this like that. Assuming you've done phases 1 and 2 well, it's now time to bring in more specifics. This is when distance, duration, sets, reps, tempo and all the other specifics come in. For example, on Mondays I will squat with X weight for Y sets. Then I will work on bench pressing skill. On Tuesday I will run X kilometres at a speed of Y minutes per kilometres and so on. This is the phase where specifics matter. This is when a traditional plan comes into play. This is when you start having expectations.

Usually, most people jump straight to phase 3, ignoring phases 1 and 2. Why? Because we take consistency for granted. We believe that we should be consistent naturally. And if we're not able to be consistent, we say we lack motivation or life is too hard or call ourselves lazy. In reality, none of that is true. What we need to do is start at the very bottom, accept that there will be failures along the way and patiently practise being consistent. Because if you want to stay fit and healthy in the long term, you need to sustain your efforts. And for that you need to master one skill, and that is consistency.

> Slow is smooth and smooth is fast. What do you think about this line? Do you think you have it in you to slow down and master the art of consistency before trying to do too much too soon? If not, why not?

#96 Moderation is an expert move

Plants need water to grow and thrive. Not a lot and not all at once. Just a little, day after day, for as long as they stand. We need effort to grow and thrive. Not a lot and not all at once. Just a little, day after day, for as long as we live.

Intensity is exciting. Scary, hard—but also exciting. Be it cramming before an exam or watching M.S. Dhoni take a game all the way till the last ball, extremes have a certain charm associated with them. So much so that most people would rather pick an extreme and exciting approach and fail than to pick a moderate and boring approach and succeed.

Fitness is a great example here. We would rather try to make a complete transformation in a few weeks or months than work on different aspects of our fitness gradually over years. The same applies to finance, health, education and pretty much all aspects of life. And there are two reasons behind this.

The first reason is that extremes are hard but fun. They require us to do things we normally wouldn't and to push hard. This makes them challenging, and the effort makes us feel like we're doing the right thing, like we're moving forward. It is an experience. The second reason is that a lot of us can look ahead in the short term. And it even feels like we can control it. But the long term is harder to predict, and we feel like we can't really commit to or plan that far ahead. As a result, the big picture, though more appealing than the zoomed-in picture when clearly seen, is hazy at best.

But the fact remains that a moderate and boring two hours of basic exercises per week for a couple of years will add up to a lot more than an intense and exciting six hours of fancy exercises every week for a couple of months.

Consistency is how big things happen. It is how glaciers are formed and cities are built. It is also how habits are created and transformations happen. Consistency is how you can metamorphose into the best version of yourself. And that's why you always need to pick consistency over intensity.

> Do you prefer extremes or moderation? Would you rather do a lot of work for a short period of time or do small amounts of work but do it consistently for a very long time? Why do you think moderation is such a hard concept to grasp and follow?

#97 Patience. Consistency. Resilience.

If you have ever owned a puppy, you would know that house-training is a hard process. It's not fun either. The puppy, who is living in la-la land, has no concerns about cleanliness like we do. It doesn't understand rules or why we need them. It just wants to have fun. As a human adult who ideally doesn't want to live with pee and poop as a part of the ambience, it is your job to train the puppy.

The first few times are going to be hopeless. No matter what you say or do, the puppy will do its own thing. But you can't give up. And, if you want to have a wonderful life experience with this puppy, you can't afford to lose your cool and scare it away either. You need to be patient with it. You need to try again, and again and again. With patience and consistency, you will learn how to teach your puppy, and your puppy will learn how to make you happy. Slowly, but surely, you will see progress.

But the process is not over. Your puppy is still, well, a puppy. It will make mistakes and, sometimes, want to understand its limits and test yours. And, just when you think you've succeeded in training it, and usually when you least expect it, the puppy will act like it hasn't learnt anything. It will nonchalantly break the rules and gift you with a glorious puddle of yellow. You can't break down. You can't say all your efforts were useless. You need to remember that slip-ups, mistakes and, sometimes, even conscious wrongdoing can happen. You need to be resilient and be ready to do the work again.

It's hard. But anything worth having is worth working for. And a life with a happy, loyal, snuggly companion in a home free of excrements is certainly worth working for. So, you need to be patient, consistent and resilient. And if you can find it in yourself to be these things, life can be great for you and for the little guy.

We're not puppies, sadly. And no, we don't have to be house-trained. But when we try to make a positive change in our lives, when we try to build new habits and when it involves discomfort, we do behave like puppies. We are not easily disciplined, we make mistakes, we push limits and we always somehow find loopholes. But if we really want to progress, we certainly need to be patient, consistent and resilient.

> Think back to a time in your life when you had to be patient, consistent and resilient. Maybe when you were working on a project or when you were learning to drive or picking up a new skill. How can you apply those learnings and behaviours to fitness?

#98 Be clear. Be confident. Be consistent.

Even if you had all the knowledge in the world, you might have still struggled to make significant changes and improve your fitness. In fact, there are plenty of people today who know enough but don't do enough. Because knowledge is just a tool for change. For it to matter, it needs to be used effectively. And for that, you need three very special qualities: clarity, confidence and consistency.

Clarity is about purpose. Improving your fitness and losing weight requires you to invest plenty of time, money and effort. Do you have clarity on why you are doing this? How is it going to help improve your life? What do you get out of it in the short term and the long term? Why is this worth prioritising even when life gets busy? Unless you have clear answers to these questions, it's a matter of time before life happens, something else takes precedence and fitness takes a backseat. So, take the time to ask yourself 'why' and make sure the answer provides you with clarity of purpose.

Confidence is about believing in yourself and your abilities to do whatever it takes to achieve what you set out to do. Simply said, you need enough confidence to back yourself. Because this is a journey of many decades. There will be many, many times during these years when you will doubt yourself, when it will feel too hard and overwhelming, when it will feel like you won't get there, when it will feel like a fool's pursuit. During such times, you need to stay strong.

You need to fight against temptation to quit and keep ploughing through. And for that, you need confidence. A lot of it.

Consistency is about doing your best on any given day, and not about being perfect every day. It is the ability to do a little bit regularly for a long period of time. Consistency is the bridge between potential and performance, between wishing and working, between hoping and having. It is what makes big goals achievable.

So, irrespective of what your goals are and how far away you are from them, if you can find it in you to be clear, confident and consistent, it's simply a matter of time before you get there. Anywhere.

> Think about your fitness goals. Are you clear about them? Can you break them down and be very specific? Assume you have unlimited time, do you have the confidence that you can achieve them? And do you think this clarity and confidence is enough to keep you consistent? Or should you work on getting more clarity and building more confidence?

#99 Back yourself

Because you can do this. Millions have done it before you and billions will do it after you. Because, while improving your health and fitness is not very easy, it actually is quite simple. In fact, it's more about common sense than it is about exercise or nutrition science.

Think about it—to look, feel and function better, you need to move, eat and sleep better. That's it.

From a movement perspective, you just need to exercise a few days a week and walk as much as you can every day. What type of exercise, which equipment, which programme, at what time and how many sets, reps or steps hardly matter. When it comes to nutrition, it is simply about eating more protein, vegetables and fruits and less sugar, starch and fat. This will improve your health and reduce energy inflow irrespective of cuisine or culture. For sleep, just get more light during the day and less light at night, optimise stimulants and get to bed early. And whenever you want to lose weight, be a little more disciplined about these three. That's it.

You may be someone who is well into their fitness journey. Or you may be a complete beginner. You may have everything you need to achieve your goals. Or you may have just the bare minimum. But, trust me, none of this is beyond you, and no excuse is worth stalling. So just get out there and get started with whatever you have.

No gym? That's fine. Start with bodyweight work. Can't run? That's fine. Start with walking. Can't get enough protein? That's fine. Start with whatever you have available. Don't like many veggies? That's fine. Start by eating the ones you like. Can't sleep? That's fine. Start by going to bed early.

Forget the specifics. Forget the results. Trust the process. Do the work. And be consistent.

Betterment, be it in health, fitness, weight loss or performance, is a process, and it takes time. There will be equal parts of highs and lows, confusion and clarity, excitement and exhaustion. The real skill here is to ride this wave for as long as possible and have fun doing it. To do that, you don't need to be perfect or your best self. You just need to believe and back yourself.

> There are thousands of people who will share their thoughts, opinions and wisdom with you. And there will always be people who believe in you and people who make you feel like you're nothing. But, do you believe in yourself? Are you willing to stand up tall and back yourself when things don't go well? Are you ready to silence self-doubt and tell yourself that you can and you will? Because, if you don't, who will?

#100 In a nutshell

Improving your fitness doesn't mean working for a thigh gap or a six pack. It means looking, feeling and functioning better than you did yesterday, every day.

Good nutrition doesn't mean eating perfectly for a few weeks. It means making better food choices for many years with the goal of improving your overall well-being.

Prioritising sleep doesn't mean lights out at 7 p.m. It means improving sleep hygiene and getting to bed at a reasonable hour.

Controlling stress doesn't mean creating a life free of stress. It means learning to acknowledge, tolerate and manage stress on a daily basis.

Healthy weight loss doesn't mean losing as much weight as possible in record time. It means losing fat at an optimal rate without losing your health or your mind.

Consistency doesn't mean doing everything perfectly every day. It means riding the wave of life and doing the things that matter as regularly as possible.

Working on your health doesn't mean pushing yourself as hard as you can for as long as you can. It means doing whatever you can towards betterment and doing it consistently.

Simple, not easy.

www.ingramcontent.com/pod-product-compliance
Ingram Content Group UK Ltd.
Pitfield, Milton Keynes, MK11 3LW, UK
UKHW020925050225
454656UK00013B/501

9 789360 453725